Loaches

Managing Editors: Mark Macdonald and Martin Thoene

Contributing Editors: Robin Lynn, Barbara McEntee, Michael Ophir, James Powers, and Shari Sanford

Loaches
Natural History and Aquarium Care

Project Team
Editors: Craig Sernotti, David E. Boruchowitz
Copy Editor: Neal Pronek
Indexer: Joann Woy
Design: Mary Ann Kahn
Cover Design: Angela Stanford

TFH Publications
President/CEO: Glen S. Axelrod
Executive Vice President: Mark E. Johnson
Publisher: Christopher T. Reggio
Production Manager: Kathy Bontz

T.F.H. Publications, Inc.
One TFH Plaza
Third and Union Avenues
Neptune City, NJ 07753

Printed and bound in China
08 09 10 11 12   1 3 5 7 9 8 6 4 2

Library of Congress Cataloging-in-Publication Data
Loaches.
   p. cm.
 ISBN 978-0-7938-0620-1 (alk. paper)
 1. Loaches.
 SF458.L63L63 2007
 639.3'748--dc22

                   2007018624

The Leader In Responsible Animal Care For Over 50 Years!®
www.tfh.com

Table of Contents

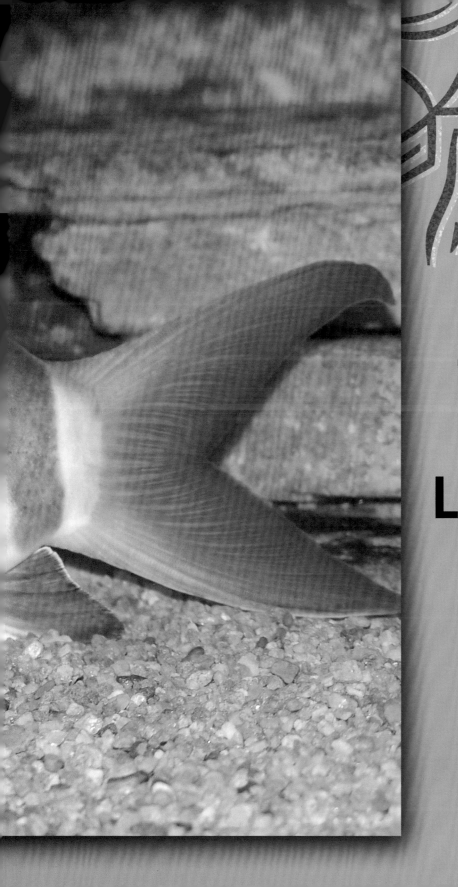

The Story of the Loach Book

Some loaches have been offered for sale as aquarium fish for decades. Others have arrived on the scene in the last few years. Still more are yet to be discovered in the wild, with new names assigned to them and much jostling about in the taxonomical and clinical world of academic ichthyology. As people enter and explore new wilderness areas in Central and Southeast Asia, China, India, and remote waterways in Russia, new species of loaches will no doubt be recorded. Loach enthusiasts will yearn for these new arrivals to eventually appear in their local fish shop.

Loach enthusiasts spend a surprising amount of their income on aquarium equipment and decor. They think nothing of adding yet another substantial fish tank to their collection, already bordering on the absurd. The fastidious and weekly labor involved in changing large amounts of water and cleaning tanks is not a chore to them, for, like collectors of orchids and other ephemeral objects of

A typical small, rocky highland stream in Thailand which is home to numerous loach species.

Botia striata.

beauty from the natural world, they will have been hooked shortly after they purchase their first loach.

Chances are very good that new species of loaches will be unveiled to the hobby on a website called Loaches Online, or LOL for short. This is the "place" that loach enthusiasts come to to school around on the World Wide Web. Like the fishes in their tanks, they go to LOL to feed on the vast store of information, for the social aspect, and to butt heads with others like themselves—curious, dedicated, a little eccentric, and passionate about these beautiful and quirky fish. It is said that people choose pets that they share attributes with. At LOL, this is abundantly clear.

The creators of, and contributors to, this book would not have come together without Loaches Online. That is to say, the website created an environment that encouraged academic and friendly relationships to develop among loach enthusiasts through sharing their fascination for and experiences with loaches. Subsequent e-mail contacts cemented that shared interest into real friendships. This book is not the only progeny of LOL, for at least one marriage has resulted from meetings that first took place there! Many close friendships have developed on LOL, and it is the source of constant discovery and the sharing of knowledge.

This book is the result of an idea to collate all of that practical knowledge and experience and combine it with beautiful images. It came into being through the dedication and hard work of people who know each other only through text messages. The editors of this book are spread across North America, and its contributors hail from Scandinavia, Thailand, the UK, Philippines, Canada, Ukraine, the United States, and elsewhere. Very few

Dwarf loaches, *Yasuhikotakia sidthimunki*. Just one example of a fish now barely found in the waters of its native Thailand. If not for aquarists dedicated to breeding this loach in captivity the species would surely be extinct.

of the contributors are professional ichthyologists, but rather simple hobbyists who have fallen under the great obsessive spell of the loach.

It is the sincere hope of the contributors to this book that our accumulated knowledge, from both practical experience and from intensive research, will succeed in achieving several things. We hope to provide the aquarium hobby with the first in-depth, authoritative resource on the subject of loaches; to offer a unique and ethical approach to keeping fishes, where the focus is on providing for the specific needs of each tank resident rather than

the traditional approach, which casually assumes that if a fish dies in our care we can simply replace it with another; and to educate readers about the wild habitats from which these fish are collected.

This last point is critical. As most loaches are wild-caught (that is, very few species have been successfully bred in captivity), it is the belief of the creators of this book that the purchase of a loach (and any other tank resident) for the home aquarium should be approached with sensitivity and with a great deal of care. Furthermore, many exquisite loaches are wild-caught in countries that do not regulate the exploitation of natural resources to any great extent. Nations like Myanmar (also known as Burma), where deforestation is a serious concern, are the natural home of a wide variety of loaches. In these places, it is individual people, and frequently children, who catch each fish that will eventually appear in the hobby. While these people earn a much-needed income from ornamental fish collection, the practice is rarely monitored, and there is no telling what this harvesting, combined with other stresses from pollution and deforestation, will do to the habitat. Without a comprehensive ongoing regulation of fish stocks, extinction becomes a genuine possibility for many species of loaches.

It is our belief that a home aquarium designed to house loaches should ideally approximate the original habitat of each fish. We believe that this will lead to successful breeding in many species, thereby reducing the need to exploit the rivers and streams that are their natural homes. By learning more about the conditions these fishes experience in their natural environments, and simulating these conditions in our aquaria, we just might accomplish a great deal more than enjoying loaches' beauty and personalities in our tanks.

Meanwhile, the authors of this book have donated a portion of their compensation to the World Wildlife Fund, with the immediate conservation of loach habitats in mind. (For more information about the WWF's Living Mekong Initiative, see Appendix I.)

So please enjoy this book and take its message to heart. Learn about how to provide not just an adequate home for loaches, but an outstanding one. And most of all, become a loach enthusiast! Check out Loaches Online (www.loaches.com), where you can meet all of the great people who worked to make this book a reality.

Acanthocobitis botia.

Introduction

by
Igor Sheremetyev

The order Cypriniformes is comprised of the superfamilies Cyprinoidea and Cobitoidea. The family Cyprinoidea includes an extremely diverse group of free-swimming and bottom-dwelling fishes. Five families of Cobitoidea contain the loach species: Cobitidae, Balitoridae, Nemacheilidae, Botiidae, and Vaillantellidae.

Many cyprinids have barbels, and among loaches they are a defining characteristic. Most loaches have three pairs of barbels (though some species have as many as four to six pairs). There are also certain anatomical features typical only of loaches, such as the structures of the jaw and swim bladder. In many ways the loach families are very similar. Hobbyists and ichthyologists alike can find it difficult to differentiate between them. The most prominent characteristic that separates the families is the suborbital spine that is typical for all Cobitidae and Botiidae species, but absent in the Balitoridae and Nemacheilidae. In some Cobitidae the spine may be insignificant or hidden deeply beneath the skin, but it is always present. Loaches have been commonly referred to as "scaleless"

You can't help but notice the barbels of *Misgurnus anguillicaudatus*, the dojo or weather loach.

The clown loach, *Chromobotia* (formerly *Botia*) *macracanthus*, is easily the most recognizable in the trade.

fishes, but this is inaccurate. Most loaches do have minute scales, which may be nearly invisible under the fishes' soft slimy skin. There are only a few loach species that are considered truly "scaleless." All the other species in the order Cypriniformes are covered with prominent scales.

Many loaches are well adapted to oxygen-depleted water. They are able to absorb oxygen through their skin and can swallow gulps of air at the water's surface and process it through their gut. Gills perform only part of the oxygen exchange for these fish. This complex method of breathing makes loaches sensitive to changes in air pressure. Some loaches become more active when barometric pressure is falling; as a result, these fishes have

earned the common name "weather loaches." The European weather loach (*Misgurnus fossilis*) is considered to have been the first aquarium fish because medieval Europeans kept them in glass bottles to help forecast the weather.

Loaches are distributed across Eurasia and a few species can be found in northern Africa, more specifically in Morocco and Ethiopia. In many natural waters they share the same habitat and are most diverse in India, China, Indochina, and Indonesia. Many endemic species have a very narrow distribution. Some species even inhabit streams in caves and become sightless in the perpetual darkness. In some areas many distinct species can be found in different tributaries of the

The loach's lifestyle of foraging the river bottom for food particles with their sensitive barbels allows some species to adapt to total darkness. *Schistura spiesi* (pictured) is a large cave-dwelling species, from the Chao Phraya River drainage in Thailand, that lacks true eyes and skin pigmentation. This loach, and all cave-dwelling fish, are protected by law in Thailand and cannot be exported.

Vaillantella maassi. This rarely seen species is unique enough among loaches to warrant its own family, Vaillantellidae. Commonly known as the fork-tail loach, it grows to about 6 inches (15 cm) and will do well in large aquaria with good water flow and filtration and a smooth substrate.

same river. The settled behavior of loaches is the reason for the evolution of so many species.

The family Cobitidae includes over 100 species. In general Cobitidae are small fishes with an elongated body. The most well-known aquarium representatives are *Acantopsis* and *Pangio* species, the latter of which includes the popular "kuhli" loaches. The more robust *Botia* are also very popular in the hobby. It is difficult to find another family of fish so diverse in color pattern, personality, and behavior.

The family Balitoridae contains more than 500 species. In 2007 it was divided into two separate families: the brook loaches, Nemacheilidae, and the hillstream loaches, Balitoridae. The body shape and behavior of the Nemacheilidae are very similar to species of Cobitidae.

The species of the family Balitoridae have specialized adaptations that make them unique.

These fish live in swift currents, so some of them are spindle-shaped while others are flat, with huge modified paired fins that form a kind of sucking organ. These flattened Balitoridae species are well adapted for living among round stones in fast streams. Their life habits are the same as those found in the small South American armored catfish of the family Loricariidae, and the spotted coloration of some hillstream loaches even resembles that of the *Ancistrus,* one of the loricariid catfishes.

There are now between 20 and 30 loach species that regularly appear in the aquarium trade. Many other species have not yet been described in the literature but are worth further study. Their diversity, striking colors and patterns, and interesting behavior make loaches a remarkable species to keep in the home aquarium.

Chapter 1

Loach Geography

Loaches are found over a surprising range of climates and continents, from Ireland to Irian Jaya, Morocco to Siberia. Members of the five loach families can be found swimming in tiny creeks high in the mountains as well as in lowland swamps. This chapter will discuss the main aspects of "loach geography," beginning with a brief general discussion of their range and then a description of the Mekong River, which will serve as an example to describe the complexity and diversity of their natural habitats.

Tropical to Temperate

Loaches generally favor shallow waters in creeks, streams, and rivers. Because of this they are able to live not only in tropical settings but also in areas that are very arid. For instance, Jordan, Lebanon, Israel, and Syria are home to a number of *Nemacheilus* species. While it is an exaggeration to say that Morocco is typical of North Africa, the attractive *Cobitis maroccana* can be found there as well.

Similarly, streams and rivers in cooler temperate zones may also be suitable for some loaches. Certain species exist in the streams of the UK, Scandinavia, the Baltics, Russia, and northern China. Overall, Eurasia might be considered the loach's true home, with Indochina the source of the widest diversity of species.

The Mekong River

One way of exploring this range of living conditions is to consider the Mekong River system. It is a microcosm of the variations in loaches' adaptations to climate, water conditions, temperature, and the rate of water flow. Understanding the complexity of the human populations that exist along such a huge river may allow us to paint a better picture of the difficulties

A small waterfall on the island of Phuket, southern Thailand. One of the many habitats in which loaches can be found.

of conservation and the challenges that face loaches in the wild.

The Mekong is one of the world's great rivers, winding through seven nations and affecting the cultures, religions, and traditions of each. Over its 2,982-mile (4,800-km) course, it grows as it is fed by freshwater rivers and streams from six distinct geographical regions. One-third of the freshwater streams in all of Thailand drain into the Mekong. This river is so large that an estimated 530,000 cubic feet (15,000 m³) of water pass by certain points every second. The variety of freshwater fishes that are found in this river system is amazing—over 750 species. Our focus, of course, is the broad and uniquely varied range of loach species.

Geography of the Mekong

Although there has been some controversy about the exact origin of the Mekong, no one doubts that it begins somewhere in Tibet. Current thinking says

Mekong River, Thailand.

Mekong River, Laos.

that the source of the Mekong is the Lasawuma stream, where it emerges from a glacier on the north face of Mount Guosongmucha. The Lasawuma stream was incorrectly identified in 1999 as the Lasagongma by the Chinese Academy of Sciences expedition. The river, known locally as the Dzanak Chu, was traditionally held to be the source. Either way, these headwaters feed a river known in Tibetan as Dza Chu (essentially, "Mekong Valley"). The Tibetan Plateau has an average elevation of 15,000 feet (4,600 m). Even at these high elevations and low average temperatures, members of the family Balitoridae can be sighted.

Leaving Tibet, the Mekong enters Yunnan Province in China and flows southward through the province's entire length, eventually becoming the point at which the Chinese border meets with Myanmar and Laos. From here it forms part of the Myanmar-Laos border, until the point at which Laos and Thailand meet at Ton Pheung. It flows into Laos from there, passing through the Lao capital of Vientiane, and then defines the Lao-Thai border before entering the north of Cambodia.

The Mekong River bisects Cambodia, winding almost due south, passing through the Cambodian capital of Phnom Penh, finally forming its delta in the extreme south of Vietnam. Here it drains into the South China Sea. The Mekong Delta is a vast flat, densely populated area. A large percentage of the people live literally on the river. The rich soil of this area is nourished by the immense river system and is the site of heavy agriculture.

The Mekong River Commission

Because the Mekong passes through Laos, Thailand, Cambodia, and Vietnam, and because each country relies on the river's riches in some way, the four nations have formed a cooperative body to manage the river and its resources. The Mekong River Commission acts to protect and conserve the waterway and its fisheries. Over one hundred ethnic groups, representing 60 million people, are affected by this program, so the commission is faced with serious challenges. For more information visit www.mrcmekong.org.

Seen in terms of the total geographical area of the Mekong river system, Laos lays claim to 76,000 square miles (198,000 km^2), or just over 25 percent of the system. Thailand comes second with 75,000 square miles (193,900 km^2). Surprisingly, the vast deltas that cover much of southern Vietnam account for only 4.8 percent of the total area of the river system.

Climate

This part of the world is, for the most part, tropical. In Phnom Penh, for instance, the temperature rarely strays beyond 75° to 95°F, (about 25° to 35°C). That part of the Mekong basin sees up to approximately 10 feet (3 m) of rain per month during the summer/autumn monsoon season. It is during the monsoon that things get really interesting for the Mekong.

So much rain falls that the streams and rivers swell dangerously. In the dry season, part of the lower Mekong is fed by Cambodia's wide river/flood plain known as Tonle Sap. In the wet season, the flow of water is so great in the Mekong that it actually reverses back into Tonle Sap and floods an entire valley. The surface area can grow from around a quarter million hectares to 1.5 million hectares. Annual flooding causes the dispersal (and frequent deaths) of a large human population. From November 7 to 9, once the floods begin to recede, the people of Cambodia observe *Bon Om Tuk*, the Celebration of the Reversing Current.

This area is thought to be one of the richest aquaculture sites in the world; it has been designated a World Heritage Biotope by UNESCO. Fishbase.org lists 193 fish species that appear in this area alone. One-half to two-thirds of the protein in the Cambodian diet is from fishes harvested in Tonle Sap.

Loaches in the Mekong

The vast majority of the Mekong is a large tropical river, but other parts are fed by mountain

Deep Pools

One geographical aspect of the Mekong River that is still being examined is the phenomenon of "deep pools." There are 58 known deep pools in the Cambodian section of the Mekong basin, and during the dry season, when water levels can drop by as much as 49 feet (15 m), these pools act as dense reservoirs of aquatic life, with cooler temperatures and lower light levels protecting fishes from the scorching heat at the surface. More information about deep pools will become available as research continues.

Loaches

The horseface loach, *Acantopsis choirorhynchus*. One of the many loaches found in the Mekong River.

streams having cooler water and a faster flow. Hillstream loaches abound in these upper feeding stretches of the system. Some of the hillstream genera found in this area include: *Acanthocobitis, Annamia, Balitora, Hemimyzon, Homaloptera, Nemacheilus, Paracobitis, Sewellia*, more than 60 species of *Schistura*, and others.

   Acanthopsoides, Acantopsis, Cobitis, Lepidocephalichthys, Pangio, Serpenticobitis, Sinibotia, Syncrossus, and Yasuhikotakia are all genera of loaches found in the Mekong as well. As with any other river, physical differences in the banks and bottom of the Mekong occur and dictate where different loaches will be found. For instance, kuhli loaches can be observed among leaf litter that collects along the river's edge and in slow-moving pools formed by such things as fallen trees. In other areas, the river passes over mounds of rounded boulders, creating areas of high water flow. This is the place to find *Schistura*, some hillstream loaches, and other tropical fishes.

   The horseface loach (*Acantopsis choirorhynchus*) is native to the parts of the Mekong that stretch through Laos and Thailand, but it has not been reported in Cambodia or in the Mekong Delta in Vietnam. The Tonle Sap boasts four species of botiid loaches: *Syncrossus beauforti, S. helodes, Yasuhikotakia lecontei*, and *Y. modesta*—but the whole Mekong supplies homes to those and ten other species.

   A river system as vast as the Mekong can offer suitable habitats to fishes with very different needs.

Many books on aquarium fishes, as well as the traditional model of the aquarium business, will refer to a fish's origin as "Asia" or "Southeast Asia." This is a disservice to not only the particular fish but also to the human cultures in the parts of the world where they originate. In the case of loaches, their collection and export may supply entire villages with seasonal income, which in turn supports conservation efforts such as the Mekong River Commission.

Tributaries found high in the mountains of Tibet and Yunnan will not be hospitable to kuhli loaches, which are found at lower elevations of the Mekong, but they will harbor certain hillstream loaches that are more at home in fast-flowing, colder waters. Within the genus *Schistura*, individual species can vary from stream to stream in the same relatively small area.

Know the Natural Habitat

The Mekong system mirrors some of the other great Southeast Asia river systems: the Irrawaddy and Salween rivers in Myanmar, the Chao Phraya River in Thailand, and the Yangtse and Song Hong rivers of China. The dense human populations and often "hot" political situations in these areas make conservation efforts both difficult and critical. As we in the aquarium hobby take part in the exploitation of these river ecosystems, the least we can do is be aware of their unique and special characteristics.

Perhaps of greater importance is the concept that, with some research, aquarists can build aquarium habitats for their loaches that closely resemble the areas where the fishes were caught. Doing this is certainly the first step to increasing the chances of reproduction in captivity. Domestic reproduction is a major goal of the loach-keeping community for the simple fact that if we can learn how to breed loaches in significant numbers, we can immediately reduce the strain on their natural habitats. In this way, one can see the importance of treating loaches (and other aquarium fishes) as more than simple "pets." It is an ethical approach, and with luck and lots of shared observation we can work towards insuring that loaches will continue to thrive in the wild and in our aquariums.

Men collecting aquarium fish in West Bengal, India. This river is home to *Nemacheilus* and *Acanthocobitis* loaches.

Chapter 2

Loach
Environment
Considerations

Maintaining a quality environment where loaches will thrive requires attention to all the details that make up that environment: the water, the types of filtration chosen to suit the loaches' requirements, the "decorations" that will replicate the natural environment (wood, rocks, plants, substrate). These elements are important and must be given careful consideration.

Water

Water is the essential element that affects the health of a loach more than any other single factor. Poor water quality is similar to poor air quality in that it *will* eventually cause illness, and possibly early death. The loach keeper must be prepared to monitor and maintain high water quality and cleanliness through regular water changes, maintenance, observation, and the occasional testing of water chemistry and parameters.

Adequate oxygen levels are the first essential for keeping healthy loaches. Oxygen-saturation test kits may be used from time to time, but general observation is the basic key here.

Most gas exchange in water takes place at the surface, the point at which the water has its greatest interface with the air. In nature, the water surface is agitated by its movement around obstacles such as rocks and by the natural flow caused by altitude change. In aquaria, we must replace natural surface agitation with pumps and filters, allowing carbon dioxide to escape and oxygen to enter the water. Some gas exchange will occur when using air-pump-powered airstones or bubble wands, but the surface area of a tiny bubble must be multiplied thousands of times to equal the surface area of the water at the top of the tank. Powerheads circulate water more thoroughly, bringing a greater volume of it into contact with the air at the surface. Some powerheads utilize a venturi system, injecting air into the outgoing water flow. This is an excellent method for maintaining high levels of oxygen in the water.

The behavior of the loaches will also indicate the level of oxygen in the water. Low activity levels, increased respiration rate, and gasping at the surface are signs that something is very wrong. This sort of behavior *may* indicate a need for more oxygen in the water but often is a sign that the affected loach is not getting enough oxygen for other reasons, including infection (see Chapter 6).

Particularly susceptible to low oxygen problems are tanks with a still water surface. This can result from water levels being too high, or filter outflows being too low. In heavily planted tanks with carbon dioxide augmentation, the plants' photosynthesis slows dramatically at night; it's possible for the oxygen to be depleted rapidly. If any signs of oxygen depletion appear, it is advisable to install an airstone or bubble wand, or some other mechanism that will both circulate the water and agitate the surface.

Water Flow Rate and Water Changes

Because loaches inhabit the bottoms of constantly moving streams and rivers, they should be kept in aquaria with greater water flow than that found in the average tank. Increasing the water flow not only serves to oxygenate the water but also prevents food and waste that accumulates on the bottom of the tank from breaking down due to

> **Keep Water, Not Fishes**
> *The importance of good water quality for the well-being of the fishes is such that fish keepers sometimes joke that they actually keep water, not fishes!*

Different loaches have different oxygen requirements. For example, this waterfall in northern Thailand is the natural habitat of *Schistura mahnerti* and *S. reidi*. When habitats such as this are shared by more than one species in the same genus, each one typically claims a different ecological niche. In this area *S. reidi* can be found foraging in the calm shallows while *S. mahnerti* favor the stronger flowing rapids. Research your loach to find its oxygen requirement.

anaerobic bacteria. Water flow can be improved in a variety of ways. Upgrading to a larger filter or installing more than one filter in the tank can prevent all kinds of problems and can save lives should one filter break down. Installing even a small powerhead for use with one or more filters further guarantees improved water flow.

Frequent and large water changes are recommended. Many experienced loach keepers find that changing a minimum of 25 percent of the water volume weekly will aid in keeping dissolved organic compounds (DOC) and nitrates at acceptable levels. Nitrates are the end product of the bacterial breakdown of waste products and will build up to unacceptable levels if not diluted by water changes. Therefore it may be wiser to change as much as 40 to 50 percent of the water every week. Sensible stocking levels in the tank and careful feeding practices can greatly affect the necessity for water changes. Provided with clean water and just enough food to thrive, loaches will be more active in the aquarium, giving their keepers greater enjoyment.

To gain a better understanding of the rate at which nitrates develop, it may be useful to monitor the tank's water parameters for a couple of months, or at least several weeks. This can help the loach keeper appreciate the critical need for water changes and to develop a routine that meets the loaches' ideal situation. Regular use of a gravel vacuum during water changes can reduce the DOC and nitrate levels by removing the sludge that accumulates throughout the tank's substrate. This is especially important in loach tanks because loaches

> **Watch and Learn**
> *With observation and experience, the loach keeper will find appropriate feeding levels that will keep the tank inhabitants healthy while maintaining good water parameter balance.*

live in such close proximity to the substrate. Most loaches will actively search in the substrate for food and even bury themselves, so a clean substrate is essential to avoiding bacterial infections.

Besides maintaining excellent water quality, a suitable temperature must be maintained. There are numerous manufacturers of aquarium-designed heaters. Generally these heaters are reliable and trouble free. However, as with most things in life, quality costs more, and paying for a good heater will be rewarded by superior performance in both accuracy of temperature regulation and longevity. Multiple heaters may be required in large tanks to give consistent temperature throughout. Heaters should be placed in areas with good water flow to assist in heat distribution.

A hang-on-the-back filter.

In some climates, excessive summertime heat may be a problem, particularly if the tank is kept in a space that lacks air conditioning. A crude form of evaporative cooling can be obtained by using a clip-on or pedestal room fan to blow air across the tank at the water's surface. The tank will require water top-offs to replace that which evaporates.

Filtration Equipment

A number of different aquarium filtration options are available. Each has advantages and disadvantages in terms of keeping loaches and providing for their special needs.

Hang-on-the-back Filters

Hang-on-the-back (HOB) filters offer easy maintenance, but also require wide open spaces in the hood of the tank for outflow. Loaches are notorious jumpers and have a particular fondness for swimming against a current. They will therefore use the outflow from any HOB as an escape route and often will be found in the media compartment or on the ledge of a bio-wheel filter. They may also leap from the tank through the gaps around the filter. The use of plastic canvas, nylon mesh, or fiberglass screening material around openings in the tank and across filter outlet ramps can prevent loaches from making a quick but badly planned escape. Some loach keepers have also used plastic food wrap effectively to cover the openings around the filter.

Canister Filters

Canister filters offer fewer escape routes around the narrow tubing that enters and exits the tank, increased biological filtration, and more media choices. Additionally, the filter can be kept out of sight. One potential drawback to these filters has to do with cleaning their internal media.

Manufacturers recommend infrequent cleaning of media, but with planted tanks and loaches it is wise to clean the filter more often. This is because plant debris will be sucked into the filter and then will decay, adversely affecting the clean water conditions required by loaches. Frequency of cleaning will depend on the types of plants in the tank, which species are being kept, fish size, stocking level, and the amount and type of feeding. This can best be determined through experimentation. Generally, tanks housing larger species such as *Botia* will require the most maintenance. Cleaning can be a bit of a chore depending on the make of canister filter being

Canister filters can be a chore to clean, but have been found by loach keepers to be reliable.

used, but it can be done quickly once a routine is established. In the event of a power failure, anaerobic bacteria can wreak havoc in such a system, but many loach keepers find them otherwise perfectly reliable. The initial high cost of a canister filter may be offset by the years of dependable service it provides.

Undergravel Filters

Undergravel filters have somewhat fallen out of vogue in recent years. While they are inexpensive to purchase, they have certain disadvantages when one is keeping loaches. While using a powerhead with an undergravel filter can increase water flow, which is definitely beneficial, many loaches prefer a soft substrate for burrowing. Undergravel filters are better suited for use with a substrate of true gravel. Another disadvantage of undergravel filters is that they pull waste solids down into the gravel. This creates a problem for digging and burying loaches because it raises the possibility of barbel or skin infections. Some undergravel systems come with holes for extra uplift tubes that may go unused. These generally come with removable caps, which should be glued in place using an aquarium-grade sealant. If the caps are not secured properly, loaches have been observed popping them off and entering the area beneath the plate, under the gravel substrate, where their removal is most difficult.

Additional Filtration

Some powerheads can be attached to filter canisters inside the tank. These are often sold as

> **Is Your Loach Stuck?**
> *If a glass-bottomed tank containing a loach trapped under an undergravel filter is mounted on a stand that supports only the rim of the tank, a strong light directed through the bottom of the tank may encourage the loach to find its way back above the gravel plate.*

units that polish the water by removing debris in suspension and are known as "quick filters." The downside is that the polishing medium is extremely fine and requires frequent replacement. If the quick filter is only being used as a means of providing additional water movement and/or an extra polish to the water, this medium can be vigorously washed under a tap to clean it thoroughly. However, if one requires consistent biological filtration from the unit, the attached filter canisters can be adapted to use cylindrical pond intake sponges, which are much easier to clean. They can be treated like the sponges in other varieties of filter— simply rinse them in used tank water. This increases both the biological filtration in the tank and the flow of water. Any powerhead used within the tank to provide more circulation in this way should be fitted with either a quick filter canister or an intake sponge to avoid sucking in plant material or, worse, a small fish.

Powerheads can be mounted in the tank as required, directing the flow of water one way or another. Two of these can be mounted in the tank to create a slow whirlpool effect, or they can be used in harmony with HOB or external canister filters. If two filters are mounted at opposite ends of the aquarium, filtration is increased and the aquarist can be reassured that if one fails the other will do the job.

Another means of providing backup filtration as well as increasing surface agitation is through the use of air-powered sponge or corner filters. These have the advantage of being able to be powered by battery-operated air pumps during power outages, thus providing some short-term filtration and oxygenation in an emergency situation. The downside of this type of filtration is that it is more difficult to integrate into a tank. One must sacrifice aesthetics for safety; apply extra creativity in planting the tank, or otherwise hide them.

Although presenting more of a plumbing challenge, sumps are a viable choice for filtration on a loach tank. Placed below the tank, usually in a closed compartment, sumps are considered easy to clean and maintain, provide a large biological media compartment, and are unsurpassed in their ability to provide a well-oxygenated environment. Usually combined with overflow boxes, sump filtration has only minor disadvantages. This is a more elaborate method for providing filtration, and many homemade variations exist. The Internet is a great source of advice for customizing sump setups.

Filtration equipment, depending on its type, plus various electrical wiring required to power the equipment, can create a visual clutter across the back of the aquarium. For aesthetic reasons and for the security of the fish, it's best to cover at least the rear and sometimes the ends of the tank with some form of background. Ideally, this should not be too light in color and can be as simple as plain black paper or cardboard, or the exterior glass can be painted with a good-quality polyurethane or latex paint. Various manufacturers also produce waterproof background materials that are available by length off the roll. These offer various plain colors, usually blue or black, plus a wide range of photographed images of underwater scenes. With careful choice, a background may resemble the decor within the tank and add visual depth to the scene that one perceives.

> **Protect Your Fishes**
> *Ammonia and nitrite may burn the gills of more sensitive fishes and cause impaired respiration or permanent damage.*

Creating a Safe and Healthy Environment for Loaches

Because they have specific needs, some time should be taken in planning a new environment for loaches before they are purchased and brought home. Whether starting a brand-new tank for them or adding them to an established community tank, several special requirements should be considered.

Completely New Setup

The advantages to the aquarist in starting from scratch are many. Appropriate choices can be made in terms of tank size, filtration equipment, and aquascaping including substrate, plants, and integrated hiding spots specifically for loaches. Some time should also be allowed for establishing healthy biological filtration. Some people choose to use hardy fishes such as danios or White Cloud Mountain minnows to provide the required waste input, but cycling a tank should not be attempted using loaches, as most are extremely sensitive to even very low levels of ammonia and nitrites in their water.

The purpose of cycling a new tank is to gradually introduce fishes and their waste products to the water so colonies of nitrifying bacteria will grow in the tank's filter media, and also in the substrate. Some nitrate is absorbed by the roots of plants and converted back into food for the fishes, completing the cycle. Hardy fishes are better prepared to deal with the toxicity of both ammonia and nitrite. In a fully cycled tank no signs of either should be present.

Cycling a tank can be done without using fishes. Rather than endanger the life of any fish, "fishless cycling" is recommended for aquarists who do not have access to filter media or substrate from an already established and healthy tank. Fishless cycling refers to a process in which ammonia is added in small amounts to the aquarium over a period of several weeks. Beneficial bacteria will colonize the filter sponges and other filter media. (Information about techniques, products, and instructions for fishless cycling are available in other books and on the Internet.) To preserve these bacterial colonies as they develop and once they are established, sponges and filter media should only be cleaned by rinsing in spent aquarium water, as the chlorine and chloramine in tap water can kill the bacteria.

Of course, if cycled filter media or substrate is available, it is the quickest method to kick-start a new setup. Filters and substrate from an established tank should be teeming with all the beneficial bacteria needed to create a healthy biological balance in the water. Using water from an established tank does not provide significant quantities of bacteria, so completely fresh water may be used. But if clean aged water from an established healthy tank is available, it can only help the new tank become established.

Aging tap water in a container for a period of 24 hours or more can be useful, as it allows the water to release chlorine and a certain amount of other dissolved gases. Both well and city water should be checked to determine whether the water is treated and whether it is treated with chlorine or chloramine. Any local water department (or in the case of well water, a home test kit) should be able to provide this information.

Both chlorine and chloramine should be removed from the water prior to filling the tank. This can be done by adding dechlorinator, which is widely available in a number of forms from any aquarium shop. If the water is treated *with chlorine only,* the chlorine can be removed by agitating the water thoroughly and aging it in a container for a minimum of 24 hours. Please note that this technique *will not remove chloramine.* Some water conditioners, available at aquarium shops, will remove chlorine *and* chloramine as well as heavy metals. Not every product of this kind is created equal in terms of cost-per-volume of the water treated, so it is worthwhile comparing and experimenting until a cost-effective and satisfactory dechlorinator is found.

Compatibility must be taken into account when selecting loaches. Some are peaceful and suitable for a community tank, but some, like *Syncrossus beauforti* (pictured), are aggressive. Aggressive loaches should be kept with fast-swimming and large fishes and/or other aggressive loaches.

Established Community

The first consideration to be made before adding loaches to an existing community tank is compatibility. Will the loaches be compatible with the fishes already in the tank and with the foods they eat? Will the established fishes be compatible with the higher water flow rates that benefit most loaches? Will each fish have enough space in the different levels of the water column where they live? Will the growth potential of the existing fishes or the new loaches lead to eventual overcrowding?

It is a wise practice to rearrange the aquascaping of the tank somewhat before adding the new loaches. The fish find and re-establish their territories while the newcomers stake their own claims. If this is not done, some territorial species can stress the new loaches as they defend their portion of the tank. This behavior can be extremely aggressive in some species and can occasionally result in the unnecessary loss of new fish.

The quarantine of all new additions to a community tank—not just loaches, but loaches in particular—in a specialized quarantine tank for a period of four or more weeks is highly recommended. This serves to screen the loaches for illness or any of the parasites commonly found in wild-caught fishes. It also allows the loaches to adapt to local water conditions without the added stress of competing with the other fishes in the tank over already established territories (see Chapter 5).

A 10-gallon (38-liter) tank is adequate for this purpose. The smaller volume allows for easier (and less expensive) treatment should a disease manifest itself.

Decoration Safety Consideration

It is not uncommon for loach keepers to be faced with the challenge of safely extracting

A Strong Word of Caution

Whether using silicone for attaching ornaments, filling dangerous holes or crevices in wood, applying gravel to PVC, or any other use in the aquarium, *never* use the type of silicone sealant found in hardware or home improvement stores. The vast majority of these commercial sealants have chemical additives such as fungicides that are deadly to fishes even after the silicone has cured. Aquarium-safe silicone can be purchased at most pet stores.

fishes that find themselves trapped in the hollows and holes of tank ornaments or pieces of wood. Loaches are naturally very inquisitive and will occasionally explore small spaces in the tank. Sometimes an item of aquascaping that was once a safe and familiar hiding spot can become a death trap for a growing loach. This should be carefully considered when purchasing decor for the tank. The needs and preferences of the specific fish should be considered when planning a loach-friendly environment. Some prefer wood or heavy planting, while others might find rocky hideaways to their liking. Once the desired material is chosen, other factors should give pause for thought.

Wood

Branches and roots are part of a loach's natural environment. Rivers erode the banks and fallen debris becomes trapped, where it provides hiding places and shade for reclusive loaches.

When selecting a piece of wood of appropriate size and shape for the tank, it is helpful to consider just how the wood might be exploited by loaches. Small crevices that allow just enough room for a loach to be trapped or wedged inside will soon contain one. A desirable but problematic piece of wood can be made safer by filling holes and inviting crevices with aquarium-grade silicone sealant. This must dry and cure for at least 48 hours before being placed in the aquarium.

The two most commonly available types of wood for the aquarium are Malaysian driftwood and mopani, a two-toned wood, also known as bogwood or African root wood. While both types benefit from a thorough cleaning under hot water with the use of a stiff brush, mopani also benefits from a week or two of pre-soaking, which helps reduce the leaching of tannins into the water. Tannins stain the water a rich brown tea color and slightly lower the pH. Small amounts of baking soda can be added during the pre-soaking phase to reduce both of these effects.

Wood can also be taken from natural streams or lakeshores for use in the tank. The bark should be removed, and the wood must be sterilized by being submerged in boiling water for at least an hour. Boiling and scrubbing with a stiff brush also reduces some of the effect of the tannins. This technique can be used for ridding mopani of excess tannins quickly. A few hours of boiling makes the wood ready for the aquarium in a short time rather than a few weeks. Boiling and scrubbing the wood will also help reduce the introduction of spores and other unwanted organisms to the tank.

Both kinds of wood will stain the water to some degree, and this can be used to the advantage of the general look of the natural loach tank. However, if the aquarist does not find the staining of the water aesthetically pleasing, the use of activated carbon within the filtration system will remove the coloration. After several months in the aquarium the wood may be given a thorough scrub with a stiff-bristle brush under running water. This will remove much of the softened exterior of the piece and also reduce or halt the tannins' effect on the water.

Rocks and Other Hard Decor

Rocks are a part of the natural scene and can be used to create form within the tank and the dark refuges many loaches need for security. Many varieties are sold in aquarium shops: rainbow rock, petrified wood, slate, and so on. Rocks collected

Avoid placing rocks with sharp edges in your loach tank.

from lakes and streams can also be used and may produce a more natural look for the loach tank. Regardless of which type of rock is chosen, avoid any types with abrasive surfaces (like lava rock) or those that have sharp edges.

The appearance of the rocks one uses is somewhat up to personal choice. It is doubtful that the fishes are too concerned with aesthetics, but one must ensure they are non-calciferous. Calciferous rocks leach minerals into the water, which will likely increase both the hardness and pH of the aquarium's water. To test for this, place a small amount of vinegar on the rock (before it goes into the tank) and if a foaming reaction occurs, the rock should be considered calciferous and rejected.

Regardless of which rocks are chosen, they should all be washed thoroughly and scrubbed with a stiff-bristle brush prior to placement in the tank. They can be sterilized by soaking in a solution of water and bleach for at least three hours. Rocks should then be rinsed in multiple changes of clean cold water to remove chlorine.

Slate is often used in loach tanks for building walls or caves because it is usually flat and of a uniform thickness. Caves can be created by stacking pieces of slate to create cavities that loaches will find attractive. They may be built by simply stacking, or assembled dry and held together with aquarium-safe silicone. (It is best not to make these glued stacks too large, as it may be necessary at some time to remove the structure for cleaning or to access a fish that may try to evade capture.) Slate is also very effective as a means of creating supporting walls for elevated planting areas. This is accomplished with a few simple tools and a quantity of slate and gravel.

The slate must be in manageable sizes. If there are pieces that are too large, a hammer can be used to

Slate Safety Tip
In the process of breaking the slate, sharp shards are likely to fly everywhere so it is wise to wear protective goggles. Be sure to have cleanup tools handy, and perform the task in an environment where the debris can be easily swept away.

split them. After breaking each piece, make sure the edges are smoothed and rounded. Slate can be very sharp when broken. Coarse sandpaper, grinding tools, or masonry files will be adequate to perform this task.

A layer of gravel should underlie the entire wall and the space behind it. The first course of slate can be laid in the shape of the desired wall. Take care in selecting the pieces for this first, load-bearing layer. Choose pieces that fit together tightly. As the wall is built it will lean slightly inwards towards the planted area; be certain that the original layer allows for this decrease in size. Try to fit each piece so that it interlocks as best as it can. Each piece will then hold the other piece in place, almost like a 3-D jigsaw puzzle. With each layer of slate, use gravel to fill in the area behind the wall and any crevices in the slate. This will help maintain the strength of the wall and hold everything in place. Continue to the desired height. When the wall is completed, the elevated planting area is also ready for the addition of plants.

With this additional space, plants of different heights and structure can be combined effectively. Multi-layer planting is favored in the so-called "Dutch Aquarium" style. Countless examples of this potentially beautiful design technique exist on the Internet and in books.

PVC Tubes and Fittings

Polyvinyl chloride (PVC) is a dense plastic that sinks in water and can be an excellent material for creating hiding and resting spots for loaches and other fishes. Fittings and pipes of differing diameters can be purchased from most hardware stores. Ensure that the components are designated as being PVC or having a "potable" (i.e. drinking) water designation. This is indicated by the manufacturer's marking system: "NSF-PW" on all Schedule 20 and 40 PVC as well as on gray plumbing parts. By connecting various joints and straight lengths, a variety of complex environments can be arranged and then lifted for easy cleaning. Unlike many wood, rock, and plant combinations, homemade PVC ornaments are easily moved while vacuuming the substrate.

PVC pipes may be used whole or cut to any desired length. After cutting, remove any fine chips and sand rough edges with an abrasive paper. PVC may then be smeared with aquarium-grade silicone sealant, then coated in sand, gravel, or the same substrate used in the aquarium to disguise its artificial appearance. When using whole lengths of pipe, it is critical to monitor the growth of loaches, particularly clown loaches, to avoid having any of them becoming trapped inside the tube.

Flowerpots

Clay flowerpots may also be used for hiding spots, either placed on a side and used whole or cut in half with a masonry blade. If used whole, it is advisable to plug the small drainage hole in the bottom of the pot. Aquarium-grade silicone sealant used alone or to hold a marble in place works well. As with PVC, the pots may be slathered with aquarium-safe silicone and covered with a substrate of choice. It is vital to only use new flowerpots. Any that have been used for horticulture may have

absorbed unwanted chemicals or pesticides from plant soil. Unglazed clay is porous and can hold these elements for a long time. It is safer to start with a newly purchased clean pot.

Substrate

All loaches of the family Cobitidae, and many of the family Balitoridae, enjoy a soft substrate in the tank. Sand of various grades and fine-grade

Clay flowerpots and PVC pipe can be used in your tank to create hiding spots for your loaches, but only if they have not been used elsewhere first. Only new and clean pots and pipe should be used.

aquarium gravel are preferred. Sand or gravel should be chosen that have rounded grains to avoid damage to delicate barbels and the bodies of those species that like to bury themselves. Darker-colored, natural looking substrates can add a visual appeal to the loach tank, and they reflect less light, thereby reducing stress on light-sensitive loaches. Some experienced loach keepers prefer the type of sand sold for pool filters. Play sand for sandboxes can also be used, although it may be difficult to thoroughly clean and may contain contaminants. Onyx sand and "moon sand" are darker in color

> **Protect Your Filters**
> *Nylon mesh, or preferably sponge materials, can be placed over the intake pipes to protect filters in sandy-bottom tanks.*

and, being relatively inert, they will not affect the water chemistry. Onyx sand may actually help to keep the water at a neutral pH because it acts as a mild pH buffer and is beneficial to plants. Sands made for use in marine tanks and sands made for African Rift Lake Cichlid tanks should not be used. They are high in salts and calcium and will adversely affect the water chemistry. Beach sand should be avoided also, one reason being that it can contain a lot of organic matter.

After thoroughly rinsing the selected sand or fine gravel, it can be placed in the tank. Care should be

All gravel and sand used to create the substrate for your loach tank should be of a fine-grade.

taken not to stir up any of this substrate while initially adding water or during water changes. Particles of sand in suspension can damage or ruin filtration pump impellers. Avoid choosing very fine sand grades for this reason.

While many references suggest that the substrate must be deep, many plants do not require this at all. When using finer sand it may even be preferable to aim for a shallow substrate depth of about 1.5 inches (3.8 cm). This can allow for easier maintenance and prevent the development of anaerobic decay in the substrate, which can be detrimental to the health of the tank.

One advantage of sand is that wastes tend not to penetrate the substrate as with gravel. Maintenance and vacuuming in a sand substrate is surprisingly simple. The gravel vacuum can be passed lightly across the surface—near it, but not into the sand. Most waste will be removed. It is useful to occasionally stir the sand to expose possible areas of anaerobic decay and to circulate the beneficial bacteria found in the substrate. This is done best by hand, since pointed objects can harm loaches that may be entirely hidden under the sand. Run your fingers through the sand in open areas, allow some time for the debris that lifts into the water column to settle, and then vacuum over the surface to remove it from the tank.

Plants

Aquatic plants of various kinds are common in the natural habitats of many different loaches. Plant matter, like decaying leaves, also plays an important role in providing refuge and nutrients for loaches. It is wise to incorporate living plants in any freshwater aquarium. They can help to balance the biological cycle of the tank by using up nitrates and adding oxygen to the water.

Loaches in particular benefit in other ways from

Are They Worth It?

Artificial plants provide none of the benefits of living plants and cannot produce the same pleasing visual effect for the aquarist. For this reason alone it is worth mentioning the special considerations of a planted tank for loaches. Beyond this point, keeping a planted tank more closely simulates the look and water quality of the loaches' natural habitat and may increase the chance of successful breeding of some species in the future.

plants in their environment. As plants grow, their leaves expand more fully to receive the maximum amount of light. This creates shade in the lower portions of the tank where loaches can be found. Most loaches are sensitive to bright light and will come out only at night in tanks that do not provide enough shade or dark hiding spots. More plants provide greater refuge and security for loaches, resulting in fish that are actually seen.

Plants also subsidize the diet of a loach. Many omnivorous loaches will nibble, puncture, or systematically remove and discard the leaves of certain plants, so care should be given to which plants are chosen. The aquarist can reduce this behavior by offering loaches fresh vegetables at meal times or select plants for the aquarium that hold no culinary appeal to its inhabitants (see Chapter 4).

Aquatic plants have a great variety of growth patterns and can be combined for a pleasing visual

Echinodorus tenellus.

Good Plants for the Loach Tank
These are plants that suffer little or no damage from loaches.

Anubias species
Bolbitis species
Cabomba, both green and red varieties
    (attractive to some loaches)
Cladophora aegapropila
Cryptocoryne species
Echinodorus species
    (attractive to some loaches)
Eleocharis acicularis
Hygrophila corymbosa
Hygrophila polysperma
Lemna minor

Limnophila sessiflora
    (attractive to some loaches)
Ludwigia repens
Marsilea crenata
Microsorum pteropus
Nymphaea lotus
Phyllanthus fluitans
Rotala indica
Sagittaria species
Vallisneria species
Vesicularia species (including Java
    moss, *V. dubyana*)

effect in the aquarium for both fish keeper and loaches. Floating plants can increase shade to the aquarium, but these may be messy at cleaning time and will diminish light available to plants below. Tall, fast-growing stem plants like *Ludwigia repens* branch frequently and provide dense shade on the floor of the tank while also offering a visual appeal for the aquarist.

Grass-like plants, such as *Echinodorus tenellus,* may be planted across the substrate of the aquarium. This can lead to a pleasing "lawn" effect and can offer kuhli loaches and other small retiring or eel-like loaches ample shelter and space for exploration. Similarly, broadleaf spreading plants, like some *Echinodorus* species, can create shady spots beneath their leaves that are favored as resting spots for loaches of all kinds.

Some slow-growing plants, like Java fern (*Microsorum pteropus*), can add a rich green color to the look of the tank and shade for the bottom. Plus, its easy care will simplify tank maintenance for the keeper. This plant is found in Southeast Asian

Chromobotia macracanthus. Botiid species are both the most commonly available loaches and the most destructive to plants. Taking a good bite out of the center of a leaf only reflects their taste for varied foods, and this will occur if the wrong plant is chosen.

streams where loaches are caught wild. It is not eaten by loaches, so it may be an ideal choice. This plant is simple to install in the tank as well. Its leaves sprout from a more or less horizontal rhizome. The rhizome can be attached to wood or rocks with cotton thread, which will eventually dissolve, or transparent fishing line that can be removed after a couple of months, once the roots have grown out and the plant is secured in place. The plant can be lifted from the tank because it is attached to an object and not the substrate. This can greatly simplify cleaning. *Microsorum* species can also survive in tanks with the reduced lighting that appeals to many loaches.

Whatever species of loaches and plants are selected, there are many variations and possible combinations that will work well. Creativity, experimentation, and patience are useful approaches to finding the balance in any given tank.

Lighting

It must be said that lighting of aquariums for good plant growth is a science in itself and outside the scope of this book. However, there is one lighting tip relevant to loaches that should be mentioned.

Vallisneria, often called val, is an oxygenating plant and will do well in a tank containing loaches.

This *Botia histrionica* is, as the saying goes, heading for the hills! Always remember to have a secure top to your aquarium to prevent such escapes.

Acanthocobitis botia. The wide range of loaches from the hillstream families Balitoridae and Nemacheilidae do not generally encounter plants in their habitats and will not nibble leaves or otherwise damage plants. Species from the genera *Nemacheilus*, *Acanthocobitis*, and *Schistura* will benefit from the shelter and resting spots that plants provide, but will ignore them as a source of food.

Several loach keepers have experimented with using low-level lighting systems such as domestic rope lighting, mounted within aquarium hoods along with the regular lighting. Often blue rope lights are used to simulate moonlight. Separate timers power the main and rope lights so that they create a transitional period of dawn and dusk at either end of the main lighting cycle. This provides a more natural progression from dark to light and back again. Most loaches will be quite active and observable during the low light periods.

Light levels, like all other conditions in the aquarium, should never change too suddenly. Switching on bright tank lights in an otherwise dark room will shock the fish and can cause obvious panic in specimens such as kuhli loaches. It is better to open curtains to let in natural light, or to otherwise illuminate the room before switching on tank lights.

Chapter 3

Tank Design

One can never fully duplicate nature within the confines of a home aquarium; the available space is too limited. What one can do, though, is build a microcosm of a natural scene. The possibilities in design of aquarium decor and planting are limited only by the imagination and artistic skills of the keeper.

Aquatic plants themselves have become the focus for many aquarists. "Dutch Style" aquaria, for example, are specifically designed to showcase plants rather than fishes. In the last few years, aquarium decor design has been elevated to an art form by such gurus as the photographer/designer Takashi Amano. When using plants this way, there is a temptation to plant too many species within one tank. The end result is a kind of plant museum. It is far better visually, and more faithful to the natural model, if only two or three species are employed.

Designing a tank meant to house loaches is a major contributor to the fishes' security and health. This alone should compel the aquarist to take time to carefully plan and execute the tank's design. While it is possible to provide the basic requirements for various loach species, it is perhaps even better if these goals can be achieved with a regard for aesthetics. Ultimately the tank owner will gain more satisfaction by putting together a combination of decor and plants that creates something of beauty in the home while also providing a suitable environment for the fish.

The fish tank's decor will be enhanced if the aquarist has some idea of the natural streams and rivers the fishes inhabit in nature. A little research can provide a good foundation for replicating the fishes' natural habitat.

Some aquarists have moved away from the unnatural feel of community tanks that may mix

The river tank provides the oxygen and water flow necessary for hillstream loaches, and it can also be a thing of beauty.

fish from several continents and follow what is known as biotope aquaria. In these tank designs the focus is on matching fishes and plants that at least occur on the same continent, though they may not actually meet in nature.

The plant and fish species that are combined with loaches in any aquarium is of course up to each fish keeper's own choice. However, below are a few ideas for "themed" tanks and suggestions for loaches and other fishes that such tanks might accommodate.

The Hillstream or River Tank

The mighty rivers of Southeast Asia start as small springs or glacial melt water in the mountains, rushing downward to form the fast-flowing, highly oxygenated habitats favored by members of the family Balitoridae. Duplicating these conditions in the home aquarium requires specialized equipment and more forethought than the usual community tank, but the result can be an environment of sparklingly clean water inhabited by lively, unusual, and fascinating fishes. The specialized adaptations of hillstream loaches and their high oxygen requirements are discussed in Chapter 9.

The high-altitude, fast-flowing waters inhabited by this family of fishes can change rapidly due to sudden and copious amounts of rainfall, which produce temporary swelling of the water volume. This increases the continuous scouring effect of the water to a greater degree and rips away at the earthy banks of the streams, raising the turbidity of the water and changing its chemistry. Fishes inhabiting these streams have to be able to adapt to rapid changes in pH, hardness, and the clarity of their water.

In the home aquarium, aim for stability. Turbid water is undesirable. The goal in creating a tank for these fishes should be to recreate the clear,

sparkling environment of the streams outside the stormy season. Movement of the water is the key for captive hillstream loaches. Yet, because of the limits inherent in home aquaria, it is not possible to create a truly unidirectional flow. An approximation of this ideal, however, can be achieved with readily available equipment and components.

In 1999 the design described below was developed by Martin Thoene and placed on the Internet so others might copy it. This design has been so successful that it has allowed several species of loaches and other river fishes to be kept, and even bred, in captivity.

River Tank Manifold Design

Powerheads have been a mainstay of water movement in aquaria for many years. They were first used as a replacement method of powering previously air-powered undergravel filters. In river tanks the powerheads are far stronger than one might normally use for a tank of a given size. They are mounted at a lower level than if used on a regular undergravel uplift tube. This gives powerful water movement at the level inhabited by the hillstream loaches. Water is taken through the manifold by the powerheads. Sponges placed over the intake tubes prevent small fishes and debris from entering while also providing mechanical and biological filtration.

Long tanks are the best choice for a river tank because the concentrated blast of water from a powerhead tends to bounce back from the opposite end of the aquarium, somewhat reducing the one-way flow. A longer tank reduces this effect. Reducing the unidirectional movement of the water is not entirely detrimental, since flow reversals will happen in nature, particularly in low-pressure areas behind rocks.

Two powerheads are better than one because they supply a more even flow of water. In the event one breaks down, the flow will still be maintained. In a very wide tank of 24 inches (61 cm) or more, a third can be used. The powerheads can be from any manufacturer, but look for those that utilize the venturi air intake system that allows air to be injected into the water flow. Aim for a combined pumping capacity that will turn over the tank volume at least 20 times per hour. In small tanks one powerhead will be sufficient if space is at a premium. Tanks tend to come in standardized sizes depending on where you live. Most balance the width and height, but the US standard "breeder"-shaped tank tends to be shallower, giving more surface area for its capacity than a taller tank of the same volume. These make ideal small river tanks. If purchasing a tank specifically for this use, look for one without too much depth, unless you intend to also include fishes that live in the higher water levels. The more ground area the hillstream loaches have in proportion to the depth, the better.

River Tank Manifold Design

The simple concept of the river tank manifold provides a predominantly one-way flow within the aquarium and can easily be duplicated with simple hand tools from readily available components.

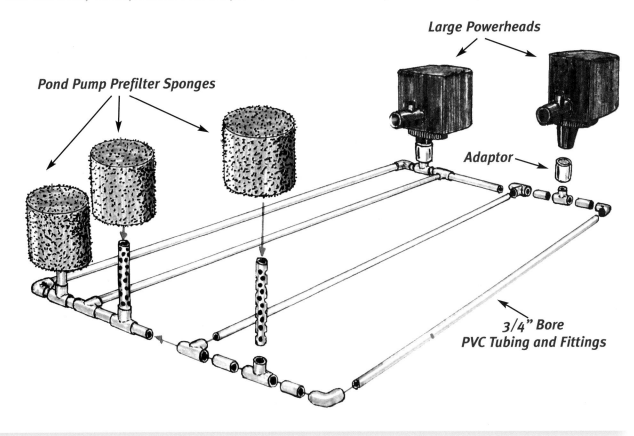

Large Powerheads

Pond Pump Prefilter Sponges

Adaptor

3/4" Bore PVC Tubing and Fittings

Setting Up a River Tank

Once the river tank manifold is placed into the tank, it should be covered by up to 2 inches (5 cm) of well-washed rounded gravel. Use a substrate with a grain size of 0.04 to 0.1 inches (1 to 3 mm) for best results. Sand can be used if it is of reasonably coarse grain. The finer the sand, the greater the risk of its being sucked into intake sponges or any other filtration systems. The intake of sand can severely damage pump impellers.

Rounded non-calciferous rocks should be placed around the tank to provide shelter for the fishes from the flow and to provide areas where algae can grow. For a truly natural look, the rocks should be similar in coloration to the gravel. This, of course, is up to personal preference and one's sense of aesthetics. Bogwood or driftwood may also be used to form an attractive mix of decor. Strategically placed pieces of slate or rock can be used to hide the powerheads and other tank equipment.

In addition to providing adequate hiding places, strategically placed pieces of rock or slate have another use. Many *Schistura* and *Nemacheilus* species, particularly the males, can be quite defensive of their chosen territory. The placement of pieces of rock or slate to form visual barriers between these territories can serve to greatly reduce aggression between individuals. The fishes do not feel pressured to defend their territory, since they do not constantly see other fishes that pose a potential threat. While the tank is being set up, rocks can be placed in a way that breaks the decor into territories, or these barriers can be placed once fishes have chosen particular areas.

Care should be taken to place rocks in a way that any undermining of the foundations by the fishes will not result in a collapse of the structure. A collapse could result in damage to the aquarium glass or, worse, a crushed fish. Losing a prized fish or having one's home flooded by a broken fish tank can be easily avoided with suitable care and forethought.

Fact
In nature, sand tends to be washed away by the fast-flowing water, so hillstream loaches are not accustomed to having it as a substrate.

Plants are usually absent in fast-flowing rivers because the speed of the water washes away essential nutrients from plants' roots. In the home aquarium, however, plants add an attractive visual contrast to rocks and will improve the water quality by utilizing waste products. Plants that have proven suitable in river tanks are *Cryptocoryne wendtii*, *Bolbitis heudelotii*, *Microsorum pteropus,* and *Anubias nana.* The latter three species can be tied with nylon fishing line to rocks or driftwood, where they will eventually gain a hold via their root systems.

Reminder
Remember that every solid object placed within the aquarium, be it rock or wood, will displace water capacity. Therefore it is quite possible in this type of tank to drastically reduce the amount of water in the system to substantially less than that for which the choice of powerheads was rated. This effectively increases the turnover rate of the tank's water because it increases the number of times its total volume passes through the manifold.

Anubias nana.

Plants, of course, require adequate lighting systems. Lighting in the river tank should be bright to simulate the clean, crisp appearance of the hillstream loach environment and encourage the growth of algae upon the rocks and other aquarium decor. While algae are generally discouraged in home aquaria, for river tanks their growth is encouraged for the benefit of these algae-eating fishes. Lighting should be at least 2.5 watts per gallon (3.8 liters) by fluorescent or compact fluorescent tubes.

Heaters are not generally required, because these species prefer cooler temperatures than most tropical fishes. The use of large powerheads at a lower than normal depth level creates a situation whereby heat produced by the powerhead's motor is transmitted to the water in the tank. This heat sink effect will usually provide adequate temperatures for hillstream loaches. Heaters will be required only in extremely cold climates to maintain about 70°F (21°C). Excess heat can actually be a problem. Prolonged temperatures above 78°F (25.5°C) should be avoided because they stress the fishes and reduce the oxygen content of the water. An open-topped tank allows cooling through evaporation, which can be further enhanced by blowing air across the water's surface with a small electric fan.

For lightly stocked tanks with large sponges placed over the manifold intakes, the sponges alone will provide adequate mechanical and biological filtration. In addition to these sponges, and for more heavily stocked tanks, a hang-on or canister type filter can be added to provide extra filtration capacity. As an added benefit, the media in such filters can easily be changed to provide chemical

Java fern *Microsorum pteropus*.

filtration. Activated carbon may be used to polish the water further.

With canister filters the return flow can be put through a spray bar to increase surface agitation. The outflow from hang-on filter designs will also provide such surface movement, which enhances oxygen exchange.

Auxiliary aeration can be provided using an air pump, either a basic airstone, a long airstone, or a bubble wand. Long airstones and bubble wands can be buried in the gravel to provide a concealed source for a wall of bubbles. Although this is not a feature one will find in nature, the oxygen requirements of these fishes mean that every source of water movement will be to their benefit. Hillstream loaches will actually sit in the water flow caused by the rising bubbles, as if they enjoy the feeling. Powerheads often come with a built-in venturi apparatus for air injection into the outflow, but when placed low in the aquarium the venturi action will not operate as it is designed. If air feed from a pump is provided to the venturi through regular aquarium air hose it will inject fine bubbles into the tank. Note that this will reduce the manufacturer's stated performance output of the powerhead.

Careful routing of air hose within the tank can reduce visual clutter. With forethought, the airline can be laid under the gravel when first placing the river tank manifold in the aquarium so the bubble wand can be supplied by a concealed source. Through the use of gang valves one pump can provide both the bubble wand and the venturi air supply. Some venturis can be noisy when using the standard inlet provided, because the outlet is open to the air. Using a closed feed from a pump and having a means of adjustment will provide tuning capability to balance performance and noise production.

River Tank Maintenance

Maintenance for a river tank will depend on stocking levels and other factors. Frequent water changes are beneficial because, obviously, the water is continuously changing by the second in nature. Normal changes of 50 percent per week are satisfactory, but 25 percent changes twice a week would be almost as good.

In a lightly stocked tank with only the intake sponges providing filtration, the sponges can be washed in a bucket of aquarium water once a month, or more frequently if required. Be sure to turn off power to the powerheads during this operation so that fish do not get pulled into the manifold. An alternative is to temporarily slip a clean sponge over the intake pipe and remove the dirty sponge while leaving the pump running. The freshly cleaned sponge can then be replaced, returning its on-board bacteria to their job of waste reduction.

If supplementary filtration is employed to increase particulate pick up and removal from the tank itself, the interval for the intake sponges to be cleaned may be extended. A good indicator of flow reduction caused by sponge restriction is reduction in the projection of bubbles into the tank from the powerhead's venturi. Many powerheads have a crude strainer built in under the impeller. It has

The addition of airstones can help provide for the high oxygen requirements of some loaches.

been found that by depending on the grade of foam used for the intake sponges, certain solids may make their way through the system and end up on this strainer, reducing the flow. One particular problem may manifest if snails are present in the aquarium. Baby snails can work their way into the sponges and then through the system to be caught in the strainer. Eventually enough shells will accumulate to cause a flow reduction. Powerheads should therefore be periodically removed and these strainers checked and cleaned, as necessary.

Hillstream loaches are not big producers of solid waste, lessening the cleaning of filters and other maintenance required with conventional community aquariums. The substrate can be vacuumed on occasion, but the fast flow of water tends to keep solids in suspension to be picked up by filtration. Build-up of detritus within the substrate is minimal. Beware of vacuuming gravel if any digging activity by the fish has been observed. This could be an indication of breeding activity, and eggs or fry might be inadvertently removed from the tank.

The Asian River Pool Tank

As rivers rush down the hillsides over rocks and objects, causing the rapids where the species of Balitoridae live, they gradually widen, thereby reducing the effective flow rate. During storms the rivers swell and rip at the banks, pulling trees and debris into the water. Sometimes these trees and pieces of debris get trapped by large rocks, and smaller rocks will be swept against them. This eventually forms a calm area that shelters fishes from the strong current. These areas are favored by many of the larger botiid species and make an ideal environment to simulate in the home aquarium.

In a larger tank of 30 gallons (114 liters) or more, calm pools can be simulated if the decor and filtration is thoughtfully chosen and placed. Rocks and driftwood can be combined with the outflow from filter units to create a swirling motion in the water, effectively circulating and aerating the aquarium. These decorative elements can also provide the numerous dark hiding spots favored by loaches. A multitude of attractive variations on this theme are possible, allowing the fishes to seek shelter or to school in large open areas.

A 120-gallon (456-liter) tank would be ideal for larger botiid species. The larger volume will give huge scope for the decor as well as provide needed space for these fishes to grow. A substrate should be constructed by mixing small rocks, pebbles, gravel, and sand—in that order—to create a flat area 2 inches (5 cm) deep over two-thirds of the tank on one side and rising to about 4 inches (10 cm) on the other side. Combining aggregate sizes

creates a stable floor in the tank that the fish are less likely to disturb. The center part of the tank can contain more fine gravel and sand than the other areas to permit loaches to dig there without disturbing plants or the other decor. In the lower side of the tank simulate the barrier in the river that created the calm pool. Build a construction of rounded boulders combined with sheets of slate. This *must* be stable to avoid rock falls. It is recommended that aquarium-safe silicone be used to glue at least some of the rocks together. This construction piles up the lower wall of the tank to within 6 inches (15 cm) of the water surface. An attractive branch or root can be lodged within the rocks so that it projects outward to the other side, hanging over the center of the aquarium. An area in the rear corner can remain open so that the heaters and any canister filter intake tubes can be

Asian river pool tank design.

hidden from view. Powerheads or filtration outlets can be positioned so that they create a current coming through and over the rock barrier, replicating currents found in the wild.

The rockwork will provide a wealth of hiding places for botiid species and also the dark shadows that they prefer. On the higher part of the substrate at the rear of the tank a large piece of bogwood can be placed to create more cover for the fishes. Surrounding this with a planting of large *Cryptocoryne undulata* or *C. griffithii* will create a contrasting area of green and even more cover. Some Java fern can be tied with fishing line to the branch that projects out into the water. Eventually its roots will gain a hold on the wood. This will create some shade over the open area as it grows. The rocks, wood, and *Cryptocoryne* plants frame the center of the tank where mid-water fishes can play as they would in the calm pools in nature.

The tank would provide an ideal home for a school of *Yasuhikotakia modesta,* who would relish

the rockwork areas. The open part of the tank might form the home of a school of mid-sized barbs such as *Puntius* (formerly *Barbus*) *arulius* or *P. everetti*. Larger rasboras like the clown rasbora (*Rasbora kalachroma*) would also make an attractive display.

Another combination in a large tank could be a group of the beautiful but aggressive *Syncrossus berdmorei* with suitably large, robust tank mates such as a school of lemon-finned barbs (*Hypsibarbus wetmirei*).

Lighting need only be as bright as required by the plants. With the Java fern closer to the light it will do well, while the crypts will require less illumination.

A tank such as this will require large weekly water changes. If it houses larger botiid species, regular filter cleaning will be necessary because of their equally large appetites. Suitable mid-water tankmates will also be big eaters and produce fair amounts of waste.

The Asian river pool tank is perfect for *Yasuhikotakia modesta.*

Yasuhikotakia sidthimunki will do well in a planted tank.

The Planted Tank

As rivers flow and widen, they slow and become calmer and are less shaded by overhanging trees. More plants gain a foothold and establish dense clumps that fishes use to hide from predators. This forms the basis of design for a planted tank.

A densely planted tank creates a biotope well suited to loaches, particularly those that experience heavy annual flooding in their natural habitats. Because of the bright lighting required by most aquatic plants, adequate shady areas should be provided for light-sensitive loaches. Such species as the small and plant-friendly *Yasuhikotakia sidthimunki* would make a wonderful display in a medium-size tank if kept in a large school. They would swim in a group through the plants and across open areas. A school of small but colorful barbs, danios, or rasboras would complement the loaches. Several beautiful *P. nigrofasciatus* or *P. conchonius*, or a big school of *P. titteya* would be stunning. In a larger tank a group of *P. denisonii* would make an impressive display.

Strategically positioned branches might have Java fern attached, giving variety to the scene in contrast to broader-leaved plants such as larger *Cryptocoryne* species, forming the main structure of the tank. Dense planting could conceal a network of gravel-covered plastic tubes to give secret hiding holes for the loaches. A carpet of *Sagittaria subulata* or *Lilaeopsis novaezelandiae* could form a low lawn in the open areas of the tank.

A tank such as this requires good filtration. If carbon dioxide is used, surface movement should be minimized to prevent rapid carbon dioxide loss. A reasonable current can be maintained within the water by strategically placing filter outlets.

On Planted Tanks

Some aquarists prefer the look of densely planted tanks. A substrate containing iron-rich materials along with added carbon dioxide and fertilizers can support a huge variety of plants. The creation of such an environment is beyond the scope of this book. There are numerous publications on this subject to satisfy the curiosity of the would-be aquatic gardener.

Loaches

57

Maintenance would require 50 percent water changes weekly and monthly filter cleaning if the stocking level and feeding regimen are kept at reasonable levels.

The Lowlands Waters of Southeast Asia Tank

The river continues on, forever spreading and slowing until it reaches wide valleys and flood plains. The slow-flowing irrigation channels, canals, ponds, and swamps of Southeast Asia are a paradise for many species of labyrinth fishes, rasboras, small barbs, and other species. The banks are densely lined with bamboo thickets and reeds, often shaded by a thick covering of trees. In these areas the water is usually soft and acidic and the substrate is dark and muddy.

This is an ideal environment for many species of kuhli loach (*Pangio* species), and a tank setup to duplicate it can be a dark, mysterious, yet beautiful

feature in the home. An advantage of this type of biotope aquarium is that it can be achieved in a relatively small tank. A 10-gallon (27-liter) aquarium will work well and require little maintenance.

Kuhli loaches inhabit the margins of rivers where leaves and other detritus collect. Here the current is not strong, so the substrate can be composed of soft materials like sand, peat, and silt. Marginal plants can grow in these areas without being swept away. One can replicate these conditions using shade-loving plants and a dark substrate. Floating plants are a notable feature of these waters and can be utilized to provide shade below the surface.

To simulate the dark, muddy substrate without resorting to actual soil, mix something like black Tahitian Moon sand with pure milled sphagnum peat moss. This will minimize reflection, lower the overall light levels, and provide a good growing medium for plants. The substrate will be most

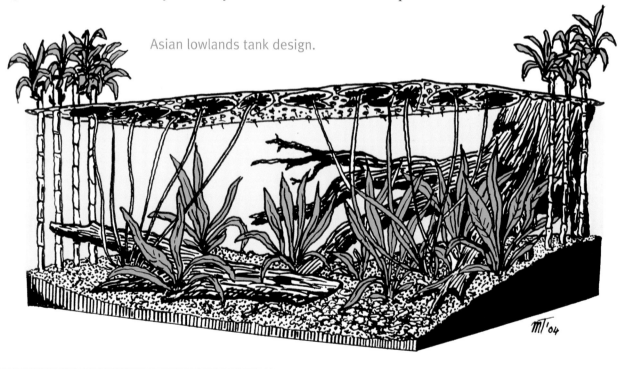

Asian lowlands tank design.

Pangio oblonga.

interesting if arranged unevenly, maybe rising to a mound on one rear corner of the tank. A root system or stout branch can be placed on this mound to represent a river's bank and used to hide the heater from sight.

Around the roots clumps of *Cryptocoryne* species that do not grow too tall and tolerate shade might be planted. On the other side, a flat piece of driftwood can be laid upon the substrate. These areas will provide kuhlis with a great number of hiding places. A few washed brown oak leaves can litter the substrate; kuhlis will love tunnelling around in them. Elsewhere, a species of *Nymphaea* lily may be planted so its surface leaves provide shade. Floating plants add to the dark, murky effect. Species such as *Pistia stratiotes, Lemna,* and *Azolla* may be used for this purpose.

Lighting is best accomplished using fluorescent tubes, because other forms will scorch the floating plants. For this reason, the tank water level should be kept low enough so floating plants are not too

close to the light source. If the tank is open-topped, a *Dracaena* species called "Lucky Bamboo" may be planted in the substrate with its leaves above the water surface to simulate the bamboo found in nature. The water must be kept clean, but the filter does not have to provide much of a current. A small hang-on-the-back (HOB) filter will work fine. As long as the surface of the water is agitated, sufficient oxygenation will take place.

Ideal tankmates for a group of kuhlis would be a small school of harlequin rasboras (*Trigonostigma heteromorpha*), any of the smaller gourami species such as the dwarf gourami (*Colisa lalia*), honey gourami (*Trichogaster chuna*), croaking gourami (*Trichopsis vittata*), or chocolate gourami (*Sphaerichthys osphromenoides*).

A tank like this requires low maintenance because the fish will produce minimal waste. Periodic washing of the HOB filter's sponges in discarded aquarium water when necessary and a 25 percent water change per week should suffice.

Chapter 4

Maintenance and Feeding

Once tank decor has been set, biological filtration has been established, fishes have been introduced, and the ecosystem is up and running, routine maintenance will be required.

To maintain a healthy environment in the aquarium, there are both mechanical details (tasks) and more subtle aspects (techniques) involved. While tasks are fairly straightforward, technique—the manner of performing the tasks—is a more nuanced topic.

Tasks

Aquarium maintenance is one of the primary tasks required for keeping fish healthy. Regular weekly or biweekly water changes of 25 to 50 percent help maintain good water quality. Vacuuming the substrate with a siphon will remove fish, plant, and food waste, reducing the number of harmful bacteria that can accumulate. Moving tank decorations and cleaning underneath them will help prevent anaerobic spots from developing.

Occasionally, tank decor should be scrubbed of any excess algae or other accumulated debris. For cleaning tank interiors, be certain to use scrubbers or sponges that have not been treated with any anti-fungal chemicals. Household sponges usually contain anti-mildew agents or other disinfectants harmful to fishes. Only sponges rated safe for use in aquariums should be used.

Before removing wood or rock decorations from the tank for cleaning, make sure that no loach is attached to it or hiding in a crevice. Small loaches, including hillstreams, may be inadvertently lifted from the aquarium while clinging to a piece of decor.

To avoid potential contamination by household chemicals, dedicated "fish only" buckets or large plastic garbage cans should be used to mix replacement water. Automated hose systems can be used for water removal and replacement. Use of a water pump with hosing attached can achieve the same results. These methods make the task of moving water to and from the tank a less backbreaking process. It is possible to further simplify the process by using a spring-loaded clamp to attach the hose to the rim of the tank and, by using a valve on the end of the tubing, the water flow can be adjusted to the required rate.

How to Vacuum Your Loach Tank

Vacuuming the surface of sand, taking care to remove waste rather than sand as the siphon hovers above it, or gently penetrating the depth with

Caution must be taken when vacuuming the substrate of a loach tank. One may be hiding in the substrate and can be injured if not seen.

hands and fingers in an attempt to loosen and oxygenate it is a much safer way to work with the substrate of a loach tank than to dig a siphon into it. Especially in tanks containing loaches that habitually bury themselves—mooseface (*Somileptus gongota*), horseface (*Acantopsis choirorhynchus*), and kuhli loaches (*Pangio* spp.)—it is wise to take the precaution of first working into the substrate slowly and gently by hand, followed by siphoning only after there is certainty that the particular area of the substrate is loach-free.

Additionally, avoid putting a siphon into places that cannot be seen clearly. Even the smallest spaces can be inhabited by loaches, and an intruding siphon may injure a trapped and unseen fish.

When cleaning hiding areas, be sure to lift rocks or wood slowly to avoid sudden exposure of loaches that may be concealed or sleeping under them, lessening the stress they will inevitably experience. It will also prevent detritus, which collects under wood and rocks, from being disturbed into the water column.

Begin to clean the tank in areas that are open and loach-free and proceed gradually to more heavily planted and decorated areas. Doing so will provide the loaches an opportunity to get used to the presence of maintenance activity in their home, thereby reducing their stress.

Technique

If a task is performed in a hurried or distracted manner, inadvertent and unintentional harm to, or even death of, the loaches may result. If a more mindful approach is taken by moving thoughtfully through the aquarium space while working it is possible to transform what could be a chore into an aesthetically rewarding experience and one that respects the tank inhabitants, causing them a minimum amount of stress.

The aquarist should strive to develop a general state of awareness of the aquarium and its inhabitants. The whole ecosystem of the tank should be observed, including the behavior and health of each individual fish, the growth of plants, and the ways in which decor is integrated to create a natural *feeling* environment. It is possible to develop a keen sense of empathy with not only the fishes but also the overall state of health of the entire setup.

Equipment

To prevent cross-contamination between tanks, any nets, siphon tubing, or containers used during water changes must be dedicated to a single tank. Alternatively, this equipment will require rigorous sterilization if it's being shared between tanks. It is very easy to spread contaminants from one tank to another through shared equipment.

When sharing equipment between multiple tanks, some suggest that it is sufficient to rinse nets and equipment in water of 160°F (71°C). Others claim

Because nets and siphons are relatively inexpensive, there is little reason to share them between tanks even under routine maintenance conditions.

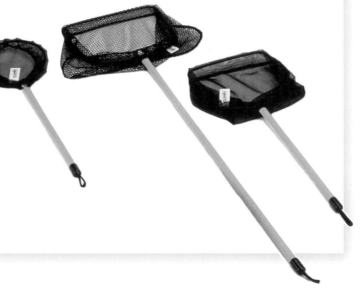

Loaches

this is inadequate and that equipment must be sterilized with a bleach solution or aquarium net disinfectant. It is an individual decision, but one that should be considered carefully, especially if a disease, algae, or snail population is present in only one tank.

Feeding and Foods

Dietary needs must be met to maintain health, encourage growth, and, when appropriate and possible, breeding.

As with many other aquarium fishes, some loaches have insatiable appetites. Their bellies can swell at feeding time, and some can grow significantly within a year. Feeding should be watched closely until a routine is established. To ensure that all fish in the tank get their fair share, loaches should be offered only the amount of food they can consume in 10 to 15 minutes, leaving no particles left over to decay in the substrate.

Loaches in the wild will feed lightly throughout the day as scant food becomes available. Therefore, if possible, it is ideal to provide three small meals per day:

- *In the morning* just before the tank lights are turned on. This provides some food for the more retiring or light-sensitive loaches.
- *Late afternoon*, after work or school.
- *Nighttime* when the lights are turned off. Again, some food should be available for shy or nocturnal loaches.

If fed throughout the day, *smaller* portions should be given. Many loaches will become accustomed to scheduled feeding and will actually beg for food. Botiid loaches, including clowns, will appear at the glass watching for the usual signs that a meal is about to be delivered. This occurs with many other

loaches and attests to their intelligence.

The food they cannot process will exit their bodies as waste. Too much feeding leads to an overabundance of waste. This waste, along with any uneaten food left to spoil in the substrate, will lead to higher nitrate levels and more work for the aquarist in terms of vacuuming and water changes. Loaches will gorge on whatever food is available and may become obese. This is neither a natural nor healthy situation.

On the other hand, a thin loach may be cause for alarm and is certainly something that should be noted and observed carefully to determine whether underfeeding or disease is the cause. The appearance of a flat or concave belly, or a sunken appearance behind the gills, is more likely a sign of illness than underfeeding. Healthy loaches have rounded bellies that may swell at feeding time, returning to a healthy

High quality flake foods can be given to many of the loaches discussed in this book.

appearance after digestion. A skinny loach, particularly in botiid species, may be showing the sign of a potentially deadly but treatable disorder called chronic wasting syndrome, commonly known as "skinny disease" (see Chapter 6).

Variety of Diet

In their natural habitats loaches, depending on their species, will feed on plants, invertebrates, algae, and other aquatic life. As bottom-dwelling fishes they mainly eat whatever comes their way. Variety is important in the diet of all loaches. Fresh, frozen, and freeze-dried foods should be mixed or alternated to assure good health and growth. Depending on the species, the loach keeper should have on hand quality flake food, frozen or freeze-dried bloodworms, daphnia, brine shrimp, or other invertebrates, sinking carnivore and algae wafers or pellets, and raw or blanched fresh vegetables.

Different loaches will feed at different levels in the water column. Many nemacheilid species of hillstream loaches will eat only food that is moving or caught up in fast-flowing water. Botiid loaches are good scavengers and will discover bits of food at the substrate level. However, some loaches are more retiring than others, and attention should be paid at feeding time to see that all of the tank residents are allowed a healthy meal.

Flake Foods

Choose a quality flake food with a variety of ingredients; many are available. Often the largest quantities are the most economical, but flake food goes stale in a few weeks and will lose its vitamins and other nutrients if improperly stored. Either purchase only the amount that can be consumed in six weeks or store airtight containers in the refrigerator. To maintain the highest quality of flake food for the longest time, it should be kept in the freezer in its original container *inside* a second container along with a desiccant packet of some kind. This prevents moisture from spoiling the food.

Freeze-Dried Foods

Invertebrates such as daphnia, bloodworms, brine shrimp, tubifex worms, and krill are available freeze-dried in loose, pellet, or cube form. All of these are nutritious, but some will be more favored by loaches over others. This form of food should be soaked in a cup of aquarium water or ground up into smaller pieces before being released into the tank.

Some manufacturers put their foods through a purification process to eliminate parasites or bacteria that are present in some food cultures. Foods that undergo such processes are highly recommended. This is especially true of tubifex worms. Tubifex worms thrive in raw sewage

Tubifex worms.

and are notorious for carrying pathogens. For this reason, freeze-dried tubifex worms are preferred over live tubifex worms as an item of diet for loaches.

Frozen Foods

It is vital to thaw any frozen food before it's introduced into the tank. Eating food that is even *cold* can damage the digestive tract of a loach or other fish. Once completely thawed (it only takes a few minutes) it may be preferable to drain off any liquid before serving it to the loaches, because some foods are suspended in unclean water. Packers of frozen foods, like manufacturers of freeze-dried foods, also can purify their foods during

> *Loaches will thrive on store-bought dried and frozen foods.*

processing; such foods are recommended.

Bloodworms seem to be the food most universally accepted by loaches, and they are readily available in frozen form. Extremely high in protein, bloodworms are coveted and may be used to lure shy fish into the routine of mealtime. One thing to be mindful of when buying bloodworms is the quality of the product. Look for a bright rich red color. Any hint of brown, particularly if it is patchy, may indicate that the product is not in the freshest of condition. Discoloration may possibly be a result of previous partial thawing. Also look for consistency in the mix. Occasionally small leeches may have been mixed in with the bloodworms.

Bloodworms. Seemingly the food of choice for loaches.

Before they are given to loaches, earthworms must first be cut into smaller, more manageable pieces. If you don't want to cut them up, skip this potential live food.

Other invertebrates are available in frozen form, such as brine shrimp, mosquito larvae, daphnia, and krill. Each of these will be received with either enthusiasm or disinterest, depending on the species of loach.

Frozen shrimp and some fish bought from the grocery store can also be added to the menu of the loach tank. Finely chopped cooked shrimp can be added at meal times in very small amounts and will be accepted by most loaches. Whole thawed shrimp can be dropped into the tank for larger fishes, but the remnants must be removed after a short time to prevent the spoilage that occurs in water with tropical temperatures. This can be an economical source of high-protein food, since "shrimp-rings" can be readily purchased and stored in the freezer to be used as needed. This food is recommended only for large specimens or aggressive loach species.

Live Foods

A wide variety of live food is available, including bloodworms, black worms, earthworms, mosquito larvae, daphnia and other small freshwater crustaceans, snails, brine shrimp, and live insects. This sort of food would be natural and desirable for loaches in their wild habitats, but some caution should be exercised when they are used in the aquarium situation. Many foods, such as earthworms, may be contaminated with parasites, bacteria, or pollution from fertilizers and garden pesticides. Any food source of aquatic origin may harbor disease. It is recommended to at least wash or rinse live foods in de-chlorinated water for this reason.

In a natural stream contaminants are washed away by the current. In a closed aquarium environment they remain and are endlessly cycled through the system. It may be safer to choose store-bought frozen brine shrimp, bloodworms, and other such food since most manufacturers of these products understand the risk of contamination and treat their foods against bacteria and parasites by irradiation.

Preparing slugs and earthworms for feeding to loaches is a fairly unpleasant task, since they must be chopped into smaller pieces. However, they are ravenously welcomed by many loach species, so if the loach keeper has access to a trustworthy source of these creatures (i.e. sections of garden or compost not treated by any chemicals whatsoever), it may be worth experimenting with these foods.

One live food that is the favorite of many loaches is the aquatic snail. Pond snails and ramshorn snails are devoured with enthusiasm by botiid loaches in particular. Malaysian trumpet snails may not be as popular, but some loach keepers report that yoyo loaches (*Botia almorhae*) will eat them with vigor. In a snail-infested tank loaches may prefer them as their main meal.

Snails should only be used from a known source such as another aquarium in the same home. They

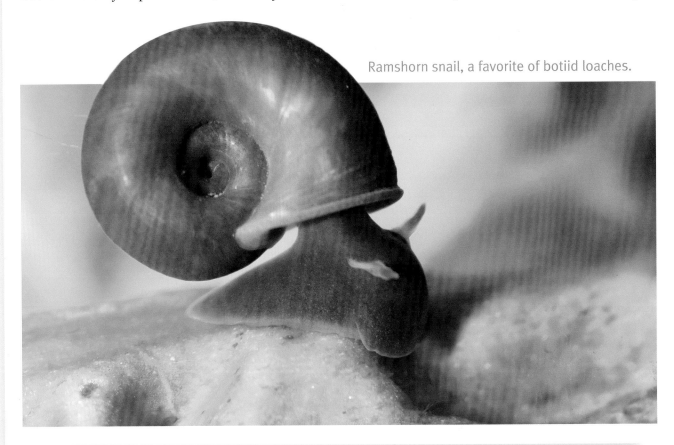

Ramshorn snail, a favorite of botiid loaches.

are one of the most common disease vectors. It should also be stressed that botiid species should not be placed into aquariums where anti-snail treatments have been used in the past or are in the process of being used. The snails absorb the treatment, killing them. If a clown loach, for example, decides to eat any poisoned snail that has not been removed from the tank, it will ingest the chemically tainted food with deadly consequence.

Cultures

Often called water fleas, freshwater crustaceans of the genera *Daphnia, Cyclops, Bosmina,* and some relatives are tiny, the largest of them measuring up to only one-tenth of an inch (3 mm) long. Usually referred to under the catch-all name of "daphnia," those of the genus *Daphnia* can also be cultured outdoors in a bucket with clean grass cuttings or a small amount of yeast provided for nutrients. Daphnia cultures must be "seeded" to succeed. The daphnia must be manually introduced into the water. Some aquarium stores sell daphnia seed cultures. They can also be obtained from a local

pond or lake. Store-bought cultures are preferable because water scooped from a pond may also contain potentially dangerous organisms such as leeches and dragonfly larvae. Harvesting daphnids from local bodies of water can also upset the balance of a natural environment.

Kits for cultivating brine shrimp, saltwater crustaceans of the genus *Artemia,* can be found in most aquarium shops or they can be homemade. Generally brine shrimp eggs are added to water containing both salt and food for the young shrimp. Store-bought kits will make this process simpler, but much information exists on the Internet for building or adapting a homemade system and keeping the water at the correct salinity for the shrimp to thrive.

Various other live foods, including "red wiggler" worms (smaller and softer than other earthworms), white worms, Grindal worms, microworms, and

Commonly sold as a frozen food, daphnia can also be cultured.

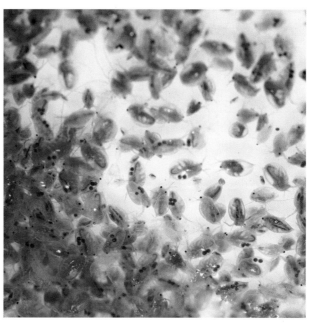

vinegar eels, can be cultivated at home and fed to appreciative loaches. Instructions for cultivating these animals will either accompany store-bought or mail-order cultures are described at length on the Internet.

Vegetables

Some loaches will accept fresh vegetables to supplement their dietary need for greens. Vegetables of the squash family are easy to prepare for feeding in the aquarium and are favored by many loaches. Sliced zucchini, cucumber, and small pieces of various squash can all add variety to their diet. Leafy vegetables are also usually received with enthusiasm.

Raw or softened pieces of these vegetables can be prepared in minutes and will garner different responses from different loaches. Slices of raw cucumber or briefly blanched zucchini can be staked to the substrate with wooden cooking skewers, attached to the lower reaches of the aquarium with specialized feeding clamps suckered to the aquarium wall, or by threading a plant weight through the piece of food.

Microwaves quickly diminish the nutrients in fresh vegetables. Briefly blanching some vegetarian choices in boiling water is preferred. Kale, cabbage, romaine lettuce, and spinach can be lightly boiled, just to break down their outer toughness, and then weighted down with stones or pinned with skewers. Many loaches, including several hillstream species, will rapidly take full advantage of such offerings.

Raw seedless cucumber slices of up to one-half inch (1 cm) thick pinned to the floor of the tank will attract many of the botiid species. Once familiar with regular feedings, some omnivorous loaches will cease munching on aquarium plants and will instead wait for "dinner" to be served.

Vegetables in the Tank
Vegetables can be left in the tank for hours, even overnight, before they begin to dissolve. Banana and melon pieces have been fed to loaches with good success, but fruits have higher water content and softer cellular walls, so they need to be removed from the tank after no more than two hours or they will foul the water.

After a night's feeding on this sort of vegetable all that is left is a ring of rind. These can be magnets for snails, if they are present, and the whole piece, snails included, can then be offered to other loaches that prefer snails to vegetables.

Frozen peas boiled for 90 seconds can be easily squeezed from their outer skin and allowed to cool. The result is a vitamin-rich sinking treat of much interest to numerous botiid species. Peas tend to roll around the tank as the loaches nibble or hoard them— the whole thing can look much like a soccer match. Numerous species of hillstream loaches enjoy the soft inner core of peas prepared in this manner.

While You're Away

Loaches can do well without feeding (or multiple feedings) for up to a week. This should not be a regular occurrence, but if the aquarist is away from home for this long no ill effects should be seen. Automatic feeders are available, either battery-powered or running on house current, and they deliver small portions of food at regular intervals. Timing of the intervals can be programmed to simulate the usual routine or one of the daily feeding times. It is recommended to deliver the smallest of feedings during times when the loach tank is not being monitored daily. Many experienced loach keepers have had success with automatic feeders.

Friends and family employed as loach-sitters in the aquarist's absence are prone to respond to begging fish with extra food. Leave clear and specific instructions for regular small feedings for potential sitters, even if setting pre-measured portions beforehand is needed. The well-meaning and inexperienced caretaker may be tempted to overfeed a tank, resulting in pollution that only an experienced aquarist could deal with.

Homemade Loach Food Recipe

For those loach keepers who want to save money and are willing to spend some time in preparation, there is a recipe for food that will appeal to most loaches. The ingredients are inexpensive, and one cooking session will result in healthy and satisfied loaches for a long time.

This recipe calls for:

- 1 cup prawns, peeled, cooked, measured, finely chopped
- 2 blocks frozen unsalted cod (approximately 8 oz., 200 grams)
- 1/2 cup boiled (or defrosted) spinach, measured after boiling, finely chopped
- 1 small can of V8 or tomato juice (or an equivalent amount of homemade vegetable juice)
- Half a banana, mashed
- 1 envelope of gelatin to set the mixture (the exact amount of gelatin required is dependent upon the wetness of the mixture)

In a food processor, combine all ingredients, except the gelatin, and blend thoroughly. Pour this mixture into a small saucepan and heat very slowly on low heat. Dissolve the gelatin in just enough boiling water to fully dissolve it all and combine with the hot, but not boiling, puree. Add more water if required to make the mixture spread easily if placed on a flat surface, but not so much that it flows.

Spoon the mixture into zip-locking freezer bags and lay flat so that the mixture is no more than a quarter inch (6.4 mm) thick. Any thicker and it will be difficult to break pieces off when the time comes to feed. This amount of liquid will fill many bags. Allow them to cool, then place the bags flat in the freezer.

Once they are completely frozen, small pieces are easily broken off. After thawing, the pieces retain their shape due to the gelatin content.

Homemade loach food is not only good for loaches. Other aquarium inhabitants will devour it as well!

Someone in your employ is likely to overfeed a begging loach if not first given proper feeding guidelines. Plan ahead and leave explicit instructions.

Fast Days

Despite the loach keeper's best intentions, it is difficult to find a balance where the fish are not overfed. At least one day a week it is advisable that the tank goes completely unfed. This reflects the availability of food to loaches in their natural habitat. In the wild some days are good while others see no food at all. Loaches will learn to feed on the natural sources in the tank like algae and food sources in the substrate.

Adding Vitamins and Medicine to Food

Vitamin B-12 can assist in regeneration of damaged fins and scales. All medicines that dissolve in water are easily absorbed by pelleted or other foods that expand in the tank. Vitamins and medications can also be introduced to the water that live foods arrive in, but care should always be given when medicating a tank (see Chapter 6).

Rejected Food

Foods of all kinds may be rejected if they are new to the loaches in the tank. It can take time for them to recognize something new as food. Uneaten food should be removed from the tank before it is allowed to foul the water. In the warm water of a tropical loach tank this can happen surprisingly quickly, so attention should be paid to this issue until a comfortable routine can be established.

Leptobotia guilinensis.

Chapter 5
Loach Selection, Transport, and Quarantine

The usual problems associated with selecting and purchasing aquarium fishes exist in the selection of loaches. But given the fact that most loaches are wild-caught, certain other considerations also apply. Many loach species do not regularly appear in most aquarium shops, and some must be special-ordered by overnight delivery or otherwise travel long distances between the shop and their intended new home. This chapter covers the process of acquiring and transporting loaches, as well as the acclimation process that is necessary to allow the fishes to adjust to new tank conditions and recover from their sometimes prolonged transport.

Diseases and Parasites

Loaches are prone to a wide variety of diseases and parasites. As with many other tropical fishes, they are particularly susceptible to internal parasites, ich *(Ichthyopthirius multifilis)*, flexibacter *(Flavobacterium columnare)*, velvet *(Piscinoodinium)*, and a less understood and

A slow-flowing section of the Kasa River, Thailand, home to many species of loaches. Since most loaches are wild-caught, it is a good idea to quarantine new purchases before introducing them to your main tank. Quarantining allows you to observe and treat the loaches for possible diseases without harming your established fishes.

dangerous condition called chronic wasting syndrome, commonly referred to as "skinny disease." All of these conditions can be successfully treated, but they are common enough to warrant quarantining each new fish before it is added to the community tank. See Chapter 6 for more detailed information on this subject.

Nearly every loach is wild-caught, so they have an increased risk of carrying internal parasites. These parasites not only can kill their loach hosts but also can spread quickly in a community aquarium. Loaches, like other fishes, protect their skin by secreting a slime coat that assists in respiration and acts as a shield against disease. The stress of capture, transport, and forced adaptation to new water conditions compromises the immune system. The protective slime coat is often similarly at risk. Because these periods of transition weaken the fishes' natural defenses, they are more likely to succumb to diseases or parasites during this time than once they're acclimatized to their new home.

Selecting a Healthy Loach

The first line of defense is buying healthy stock. Purchasing loaches or any fishes should not be done hastily. Taking time to observe the loaches in the store is important. Observe the behavior of every fish in the tank. A loach actively searching for food is a good sign, while inactivity and labored breathing are not.

The general activity level of all the fishes in the tank can reveal a great deal. Note particularly shy fishes or fishes that are showing signs of weakness. Examine carefully fishes that are hiding or are thinner than their tankmates, possibly with a concave belly. Such a fish may show signs of victimization, including scar marks on the body or fins that are damaged. Look carefully at the body of each fish. Are the fins held erect, free of

damage, or are they fraying, exhibiting signs of disease? Are the eyes clear and mouths and gills normal for their species?

Finally, note whether *any* fish in the tank is showing signs of disease. Often it is possible to see tiny white dots of ich on an individual or several fishes in the tank. If ich is present in the tank it is best to wait to purchase a fish until after the shop has treated the tank inhabitants and all signs of ich are gone for at least four days. Waiting to buy until after the treatment of the fishes will help avoid the purchase of a potentially infected fish.

Selecting Hillstream Loaches

Hillstream loaches are stocked by shops because they are available and unusual, which means they sell. They are specialized fishes in both habits and aquarium requirements.

When purchasing new hillstreams, the prospective purchaser should check for obvious signs of disease, as with any other fishes. Hillstream loaches, particularly the sucker-bodied species, have one particular disease problem that manifests itself as patchiness in their coloration, loss of appetite, and lethargy. It can come on rapidly in an otherwise healthy fish and quickly lead to death. If any fish in the tank is patchy in coloration, it is best to put off the purchase.

Look for active, evenly-colored fishes that appear to be grazing on the glass or tank decor, obviously searching for food. Rapid breathing is one sign of distress, but lethargy in a fish that seems to be breathing normally may mean low oxygen levels in the tank, which can be detrimental over long periods.

Capturing Hillstream Loaches

Catching hillstream loaches in a decorative aquarium is not going to be easy, because most decorative tanks will contain a lot of decor or plants. Well-designed aquariums provide numerous hiding places and escape routes for these fast-moving and highly evasive fishes. In bare store tanks hillstreams tend to use their natural ability to stick to smooth surfaces as their primary means of evading capture. Their best defense is the aquarium glass itself; they will attach themselves to it and stubbornly refuse to let go, even if slid up out of the water. Different species vary in the doggedness with which they maintain this tactic, but generally the more compressed species are best at sticking like glue.

This natural ability can be used to the advantage of the person who is catching the fish. Once stuck to the glass, the intended captive tends to stay still or moves by shuffling along the surface. The fish can usually be encouraged to move up near the water's surface, where its only escape route is down towards a strategically placed net.

If one slides a plastic credit card down the glass from above, gently pushing against the fish's fins, it

Gastromyzon punctulatus. Attempts to force a net under this hillstream loach carry a high risk of damage to the fins or the fish's body, which can result in possible infection.

Yasuhikotakia modesta, its suborbital spines extended. If transporting such species keep in mind that these spines can easily puncture bags. Two or three layers of bag should be used to avoid leaks and water loss.

will cause the fish to lose suction and flick itself off the glass towards the net. It is best to position the net so that much of it is towards the front of the fish, as these loaches tend to leap down and forward at the same time. The net can then be moved upwards as the fish lets go, thereby lifting the captured hillstream from the tank.

Using this method, it is possible to catch the fish quickly and without damage, meaning that these fishes, which are already stressed by wild capture and transport, have one less stressor to deal with.

Taking care during capture at the store can lead to an easier transition into a captive environment and a longer life for the fish. The new hillstream owner takes home a less stressed and damaged fish, and even reduces trauma to fishes that remain in the dealer's tank.

Transportation

In some situations loaches may not be available locally and must be ordered via overnight delivery or otherwise transported for several hours to reach

Syncrossus sp. Quarantining is an exercise in risk management. While it does decrease the possibility of introducing disease into an established tank, there is no guarantee that it will prevent it entirely.

their destination. This can be done safely if a few precautions are taken to maintain the physical needs of the fish.

- If possible, arrangements should be made so that the fishes are not fed for 24 hours before they are transported. This helps to reduce their waste output and keep down the subsequent ammonia level in the water.
- When packing the fish more air and less water are preferable in the bag. A ratio of 80 percent air to 20 percent water will ensure that the available oxygen will not be depleted while the fish are en route.
- Limit the number and size of fish in each bag.
- Bags should be placed flat, rather than upright, in a heavy rigid foam board box with a tight-fitting lid. Packing multiple bags into this kind of container will help to maintain a steady temperature. Be sure that the fish are not caught in the corners of the bag. Another way of ensuring that fishes do not get trapped is to tape the corners of the bag, effectively removing the pointed corner area. Laying bags

horizontally provides each fish with more space. It also allows a greater surface area between the water and the available air, increasing gas exchange and oxygenation of the water.

- During cold weather the transport vehicle should be kept as warm as possible. During hot conditions the reverse is true, but the vehicle should still be comfortably warm. Do not allow air conditioning to make the vehicle too cold.
- Once the fishes have arrived at their destination each transport bag should be floated in the aquarium to adjust the temperature of the water in the bag. This period will be less stressful for the fish if the tank lights are turned off.

From Bag to Quarantine Tank

Minimizing inclusion of water from the transport bag into the quarantine tank is one way of reducing possible infection vectors. The following method is a good way to acclimate a fish to a quarantine tank's water conditions.

The bag containing the new fish is emptied into a waterproof container or specimen box below the water level of the tank. Using a length of aquarium air line, water from the quarantine tank is slowly siphoned into the container. Once a flow of water is established an airline clamp can be adjusted to regulate the water flow to a slow drip, or the tubing can be pinched or tied to slow the flow. The acclimation period can take an hour or more. It is important to maintain as steady a temperature as possible during this process. The container should either be wrapped in a towel for insulation or, as with a specimen box, hung over the edge floating inside a tank.

Using a pH test kit throughout the process, the aquarist can determine when the water in the container has approached the pH of the water in the tank. Providing such a long transition period reduces stress upon the fish by reducing the chances of osmotic shock.

Once the transport water has mixed thoroughly with tank water the fish can be netted and placed into the quarantine tank. The vast majority of harmful bacteria or parasites will be left in the container and that water can be discarded.

If the fishes have traveled for many hours, the level of ammonia in the transport water may be high. If so, the previously described acclimation system can be dangerous, because as the water's pH increases and more oxygen enters the water through agitation, the ammonia actually becomes more toxic to the fish. In this case, once the temperature in the transport bag has been adjusted to that of the tank, the contents of the bag should be poured through a net into a bucket, catching the fish, which can then be added to the tank. The water from the transport bag should be discarded. The sudden change in water will likely cause some shock to the fishes, and they may initially become inactive as their bodies adjust to the new water chemistry, but most fishes will survive the shock better than the ammonia.

To ameliorate the shock effect, the pH of the transport water can be measured and then pH buffers can be added to the quarantine tank prior to adding the fish in order to bring the chemistry of both water sources closer together. The pH in the quarantine tank can then be altered gradually over a few weeks to match that of the intended permanent home.

Quarantine

All newly acquired loaches should be quarantined for at least four to six weeks. Any new addition to the loach tank of any species should go through a similar period. The quarantine period will allow the aquarist to be fairly certain that no

Keep Equipment Separate

One risk that must be avoided at all costs is cross-contamination via fish-keeping equipment. Any nets, siphon tubing, or containers used during water changes must be dedicated to either the quarantine or the community tank. Alternatively, this equipment will require rigorous sterilization if it's being shared between tanks. Such equipment is quite inexpensive, so it is highly recommended that the aquarist use dedicated equipment for each tank. It is also possible to cross-infect another aquarium by merely using the same hand towel to dry one's hands during tank servicing. Obviously, washing one's hands between tanks is to be encouraged even with multiple established tanks to minimize any possibility of contamination.

harmful pathogens will be entering the community tank. Water itself can be contaminated when it arrives from the aquarium store. Even in small amounts it can expose a tank to a host of unpleasant and even fatal microscopic bacteria or protozoan parasites. The value of a quarantine tank cannot be stressed enough. If used correctly there is minimal risk that the aquarist will ever infect a healthy tank.

The Quarantine (Hospital) Tank

It may seem unnecessary to maintain an extra fish tank that has no permanent residents and no real decorative value. However, it is very useful (if not crucial) to have one ready at all times. Not only does it allow for a healthy transition from the store to the community aquarium, but also if a fish should become sick or injured for any reason—and this does happen—treatment and observation of the ailing aquatic patient are simplified.

Damage to a weather loach (*Misgurnus anguillicaudatus*) caused during transport. This kind of wound should be treated in the quarantine tank to prevent infection.

The quarantine tank usually is a 10-gallon (37-liter) aquarium, although a larger tank may be a good option for larger loaches or groups of fishes. The relatively small size of a quarantine tank makes the process of cleaning and changing water much less work.

Keeping a bare tank with a mature cycled filter and a few hiding places allows for easier observation and cleaning, both of which are crucial when quarantining or treating a sick fish. Hiding places like the ones described in Chapter 3 will provide a quarantined fish with a sense of security and reduce its general stress. However, any decorations should be easy to remove from the tank, easy to sterilize, and of a design that prevents fishes from becoming trapped inside.

The quarantine tank does not need to be lighted. If there are no plants there is no real reason to add bright light that might add unnecessary stress for the fishes. A heater is essential, particularly when treating certain conditions that require an increased temperature. Keep in mind that whatever type of filtration is utilized it should not contain activated carbon, since the carbon will remove most medications, if medications are used.

Most loaches will be happy in a quarantine tank that has gentle water movement. If quarantining hillstream loaches, consideration must be given to their high oxygen requirements. The addition of supplementary aeration or a small powerhead for water movement is highly recommended for hillstreams.

While the sparse tank may be ideal for quarantine, the process can be undertaken in a fully decorated tank. This kind of environment will be less stressful for the loach, but it can complicate observation and treatment. If medications are called for, the plants may suffer. On the other hand, a tank with a mature substrate will maintain biological filtration more easily. This is an important consideration, since some medications will compromise the effectiveness of a tank's biological filter.

Once the successfully quarantined fishes are moved to their permanent home, the effectiveness of the biological filtration within the quarantine tank will gradually degrade. A quarantine tank will maintain an effective level of biological activity only if there is an actual input of waste from fishes.

There are two ways to get around this problem. The tank can have permanent residents in the form of two or three inexpensive hardy fishes such as zebra danios (*Danio rerio*) or White Cloud Mountain minnows (*Tanichthys albonubes*). Their waste will prompt and sustain biological filtration in the tank, but they must survive exposure to their own ammonia and its byproducts. Some aquarists take issue with unnecessarily putting even hardy fishes in harm's way for the sake of convenience, so the subject of "fishless cycling," the second method, has been given much attention (see Chapter 2).

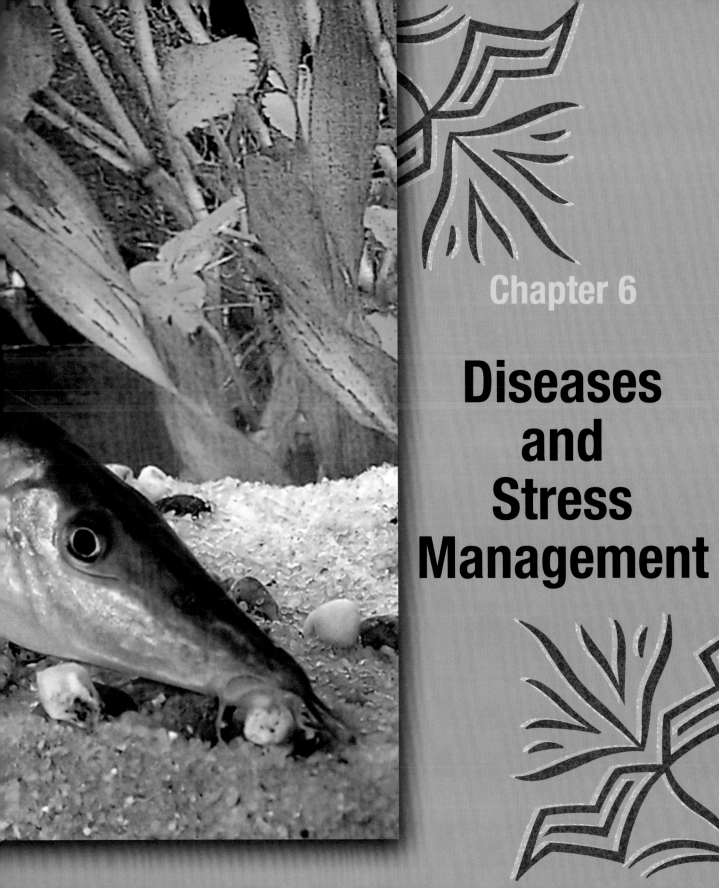

Chapter 6

Diseases and Stress Management

Like all other living things, loaches are prone to many diseases and other health risks throughout their lives. While there is little the aquarist can do to remedy heart attack, stroke, and cancer in fishes, certain harmful influences can be controlled or minimized. In captive fishes the most obvious risk to their health comes from stress. Stress has an immediate and negative impact on the immune system. Any fish with a weakened immune system has diminished natural defenses against infection by parasites, fungus, or bacterial and viral diseases. Stressful conditions for loaches include poor water quality, inadequate diet, too many or too few tankmates, aggressive tankmates, lack of security, and inappropriate lighting or décor.

From time to time, a loach will succumb to disease or parasites despite the best efforts of its keeper. This chapter explains how to identify the most common health problems when they emerge and discusses how to minimize risk of infection in the first place.

Observation is Paramount

With most illnesses, early detection can simplify the treatment process and increase the rate of success. It is useful to monitor the health of all loaches in the aquarium environment and to become familiar with signs of distress or illness. These signs may manifest as poor energy levels, loss of appetite, labored breathing, changes to the skin or fin appearance, unusual coloration, frantic swimming, scratching against surfaces (or "flashing" as it is commonly known), sunken features behind the gill area, and a sunken or swollen belly profile. Observation is the key to detecting early signs of discomfort or disease in aquarium fishes. Over time this becomes second nature as the loach keeper recognizes the fishes'

Medications
There are several medications available that can be used to treat your loaches if they fall ill. Be sure to research the medication extensively and consult your veterinarian before purchasing any. Articles about these medications and their correct uses (and also their legislation) can be found at Loaches Online, www.loaches.com.

normal behavior and appearance. Vigilant observation is the easiest way to ensure the maintenance of a healthy environment for loaches at all times.

Internal Parasites

Internal parasites can cause severe and irreversible damage to a loach's intestinal walls and other organs. This diminishes the animal's ability to absorb nutrients and harms the immune system, increasing the chance of secondary infection from bacteria, fungus, or external parasites like ich (*Ichthyopthirius multifiliis*) and velvet (*Piscinoodinium* sp.). Loaches may appear healthy for as much as several months but may then become thin and lethargic, sometimes refusing to eat. Such signs are very often the fault of internal parasites that either arrive with the fish from its wild habitat or are introduced at some point between collection and the aquarium.

Internal parasites include tapeworms, roundworms, nodular worms, and threadworms—*Trichostrongylus, Cooperia, Nematodiius, Bunostomum, Capillaria, Camallanus, Gyrodactylus, Dactylogyrus, Oesophasgostomum,* and *Chabertia*—to name just a few. Often with worm infestations the fish's anal area may appear swollen and worms may be visible hanging from the anus.

White Spot a.k.a. Ich

Clown loaches (*Chromobotia macracanthus*) are famously susceptible to this external parasite, which also affects other tropical fishes. It is highly contagious and will rapidly infect an entire aquarium. It must be dealt with quickly and carefully. Fishes with very fine scales, such as loaches, will exhibit extreme discomfort during ich infestation, and if it is not treated immediately many may die.

This protozoan parasite inhabits the water column and is most often introduced to a tank by an infected fish or a previously contaminated water source. The first and most obvious symptom of ich is the appearance of tiny white dots on the body and fins of the host fish. The condition has been described as having the appearance of salt or sugar

Here, a healthy clown loach swims contently. However, if your clown looks as if it has been sprinkled with grains of salt, it is probably suffering from ich. Quarantine and treat the fish immediately.

granules scattered over the body of the affected fish. Understanding the life cycle of this parasite is the key to safely eradicating it from the aquarium. Ich is perhaps the most common complaint of new loach keepers; it is often disastrous to whole aquaria if its life cycle is not understood.

There are three phases to the ich life cycle: trophont, tomont, and theront.

The trophont phase is evidenced by the appearance of the tiny white spots on the affected fish. The spots are a result of scarring caused by the parasite as it burrows into the outer surface of the fish. These become covered with mucus, and beneath each spot the invader forms a cyst where it multiplies by cell division. At this stage of the life cycle the parasite is impervious to any medication that will not kill the host as well.

The tomont phase begins as the parasite breaks through the skin and falls into the water column, quickly forming a sticky encapsulation that enables it to attach itself to any surface in the aquarium, including the walls of the tank, decorations, and the substrate. In the very short time between leaving the fish and forming the encapsulation a few parasites may be killed by medication. However, this period is so brief that the number of parasites actually eliminated is insignificant.

Once the encapsulation has formed, the parasite reproduces by dividing itself many times until once again it breaks out of its protective covering. At

As the temperature rises, the population of ich organisms in the tank increases very rapidly. If the water temperature is increased treatment should begin immediately. While increasing the temperature will accelerate the treatment process, there is also the danger of increased stress upon the loaches and other tank inhabitants. When using elevated temperatures as part of a treatment protocol it is advisable to use an airstone or powerhead to promote water surface agitation and increase oxygenation.

this time thousands of parasites swarm out in search of a host. This final stage of free-swimming cells represents the theront phase; it is during this phase that ich can be most easily killed with medication. Ich cells in the theront phase are not visible to the naked eye. Too many aquarists make the mistake of assuming ich has been eradicated from the tank because it can no longer be seen. The aquarist should remember that ich is still present in the tank for several days after all visible signs have disappeared.

The theront phase lasts only two days at elevated temperatures of 86°F (30°C), and four days at tank temperatures of 80° to 82°F (26.6° to 27.7°C). If in that time period the theronts cannot find a new host fish to infect they will die, but if a new host is found, re-infection occurs and a further increase in the ich population takes place.

Raising the temperature of the aquarium accelerates the ich life cycle so that the organisms more rapidly reach the treatable stage. Similarly, if the water is kept cooler the life cycle takes place more slowly and the treatment will take substantially longer.

The aggressive nature of the ich parasite can be most easily understood when one realizes that from each single tomont seen on a fish up to 1,000 theronts may result. It is also worth noting that one of the most frequent and desirable locations for ich parasites are the gill filaments. Since water laden with theronts passes over them constantly during fish respiration, in some cases ich may be well established in the gills before any appear on the body of the fish. Because of the delicate structure of gill lamellae, ich trophonts can cause irreversible damage. Although the fish may be cured of ich, its respiration may be compromised for the rest of its life.

Natural Ich Treatments

Ich is the most common illness that affects fish. To treat it you need a high-quality ich medication found at your local fish store, aquarium-grade salt, and heat.

Salt

Aquarium or kosher salt with no additives whatsoever can be used to kill ich through osmosis, that is, by dehydrating the parasite. (Ordinary table salt is not suitable for this treatment.) All fishes in the aquarium must be able to tolerate the level of salt required for this treatment option. Salt treatment may be entirely unsuitable for kuhli loaches and hillstream loaches. It has been reported that 2.5 teaspoons per gallon (3.8 liters) added gradually over a three-day period with the temperature at 80°F (26.6°C) has successfully treated the horseface (*Acantopsis choirorhynchus*) and zebra (*Botia striata*) loaches. Keeping the ich life cycle in mind, the salt must remain in the tank with the temperature elevated for four days after all visible symptoms are gone. Then the temperature must be gradually reduced and salinity decreased over several days through large water changes. If salt is chosen as a treatment for ich, its effects on various loach species and also on any plants in the tank should be researched thoroughly by the aquarist before use.

Heat

In many cases an elevated temperature above 86°F (30°C) often leads to an environment too hostile for the ich to survive or reproduce at all. When using temperatures this high it is not necessary to use medication. Because available oxygen is already decreased at higher temperatures, the addition of medications will frequently increase this effect. Extra oxygenation provided by an airstone or powerhead is needed. Daily water changes with careful vacuuming of the substrate are advised. Replacement water should be treated to remove chlorine and chloramine, if present, and must match the temperature of the water in the tank.

Be sure that your tank inhabitants can handle temperatures this high before attempting to use elevated temperature as a treatment. Close observation of the tank is necessary, as many

Ich magnified under a microscope.

fishes, plants, and invertebrates cannot tolerate temperatures in this range. High temperatures may also increase the risk of fish succumbing to opportunistic bacteria such as flexibacter.

Flexibacter

This deadly bacterium (*Flavobacterium columnare*) is also known as cotton wool disease, saddleback disease, black molly disease, or columnaris. When seen under the microscope the bacteria grow in columns, one on top of the other.

Severe and sudden or slow and relentless, flexibacter is a devastating gram-negative bacterium. If treatment is to be effective it must be started quickly and aggressively. Even with immediate identification and treatment, infection can progress so rapidly that a fish can succumb within 24 hours of visible onset.

Although often confused with fungus, fungus primarily grows on dead tissue at the site of wounds or on food that has been in the tank too long. In contrast, flexibacter presents itself on the body or fins of the fish and, most dangerously, on the gill filaments. Always present in the water of the aquarium, flexibacter is primarily an opportunistic infection that attacks old, sick, or otherwise stressed fish.

More serious attacks of flexibacter occur in hard basic water and are often accompanied by a rise in water temperature, but infections can occur under any of the previously mentioned conditions. Flexibacter infection can be extremely contagious and, if possible, all affected fishes should be removed to a quarantine tank for treatment.

There are four strains of flexibacter, each with varying degrees of virulence. Depending upon which strain attacks the fishes, they may die within hours or, with a less virulent strain, may take several days. Because of flexibacter's ability to kill quickly and to spread rapidly throughout the aquarium, it is essential to recognize the symptoms and treat the infection aggressively as soon as it has been discovered.

Signs of flexibacter infection include:
- Mouth "fungus," which appears as fuzzy lesions that erode the mouth
- Septicemia—red streaks in the body and fins, or the overall body color may appear more pink or reddish than normal
- Fuzzy patches on the body or areas on the body where the skin sloughs off
- Fins disintegrate and may appear to melt at the edges

Affected areas may appear as either white or yellow-brown lesions on the skin. Early stages of infection may appear as a dull round or oval area that is slightly paler than the surrounding area. It

Toxic Ingredients

The components of some medicines are highly toxic, not only to loaches but also to people as well. Some regions have limited the sale of these products because of their perceived toxicity to humans. All of the available formulas should be handled and dosed carefully. They are safe only if they are administered and stored properly. Thorough hand washing is recommended after each contact with the medication or the container in which it is stored.

may appear as a band that extends nearly around the body, usually near the dorsal fin, though it can appear anywhere.

Treatment for Flexibacter

Although one may try feeding medicated foods, often an infected fish has stopped eating, so treatment through the water column may be the only option. When using any medications, even medicated food, it is essential to watch the water parameters, since some will also kill the biological filter's good bacteria as well as the disease bacteria.

Because the organism multiplies more rapidly at higher temperatures, a temperature of less than 77°F (24°C) is often recommended. This may be too low for many loaches, so maintaining a temperature that is as low as possible without adding stress is advised. Increased oxygenation and good water movement will also assist in creating a hostile environment for flexibacter.

Chronic Wasting Syndrome a.k.a. "Skinny Disease"

One of the most devastating and insidious killers of loaches, particularly botiid species, is a wasting disease that may become obvious only months after a loach has been integrated into the home aquarium. A loach affected by chronic wasting syndrome (CWS) will develop concave or sunken areas, most noticeably between the eyes and gills and along the base of the dorsal fin. The belly is not rounded or healthy looking and the whole body of the fish will take on an emaciated quality, even in specimens that continue to eat normally. This process of wasting is known as cachexis.

No single cause has yet been isolated for this

The clown loach above shows clear signs of chronic wasting syndrome, sometimes called "skinny disease." Although a loach in this condition is severely compromised, it should be removed to a hospital tank and treated immediately. Full recovery is possible.

condition, though bacteria are highly suspected. It appears to be caused by one or more opportunistic pathogens during a time of physical stress that results in immune depression and overwhelming infection. It can also be caused by the introduction of a new pathogen to which the fish has no immunity. It is infectious in the sense that most potentially pathogenic organisms will spread easily from one fish to another in a closed system like an aquarium. In the wild the concentration of pathogenic organisms is very low. Fishes harbor all sorts of organisms but usually at low enough levels that they do not cause fatality.

Many microbes inhabit the bodies of fishes but are kept in balance by a competent immune system. If fishes are exposed to extreme stress their immune system becomes compromised. The microbial environment inside the body of the fish becomes unbalanced in favor of the microbes and eventually

Look for CWS

Occasionally, one of a group of loaches purchased at the same time will simply not increase in size at the same rate as the others. Some imported shipments of loaches will include many specimens with CWS. It is prudent to avoid fishes from this sort of situation and wait until a healthier-looking batch is offered.

the fish dies. It is advantageous for a parasite residing in or on fish to have a long relationship with its host. It is not in its best interest to destroy the host. However, when conditions are detrimental to the integrity of the fish, parasites kill their host and by doing so break their own life cycle. It's a lose-lose situation.

Raising the tank's temperature to combat ich is not recommended for cool-water fishes such as the Balitoridae or weather loaches, such as this *Misgurnus anguillicadatus*.

Magnified oodinium protozoans. *Piscinoodinium* is harder to kill than ich and is more tolerant of salt and high temperatures. It also has a longer free-swimming period of up to several days before it must find a host.

Treatment of Chronic Wasting Syndrome

Loaches suspected of suffering from CWS have been treated with a variety of medications, usually with good success. Informed employees of fish shops and fellow loach keepers on the Internet should be able to recommend locally available brands of these medications.

Velvet a.k.a. Rust, Gold Dust Disease

A parasitic disease (*Piscinoodinium limneticum* in North America, *P. pillulare* in Europe) caused by a dinoflagellate organism, velvet (*oodinium*) is somewhat similar to ich in its life cycle and symptoms although it is much more difficult to identify with the naked eye. It is equally contagious, even affecting larval amphibians. Like ich it can cause necrosis in gill tissues, leaving permanent damage and respiratory insufficiency even after treatment.

The different species of *Piscinoodinium* attack freshwater fishes in the same way by penetrating the skin and gill filaments where the parasite feeds and grows. Mature trophonts drop off the fish and, like ich, enlarge and encyst to form the tomont phase. Each tomont spends between three to five days at normal aquarium temperatures where within the cyst they reproduce by binary fission into 256 motile dinospores. Free-swimming dinospores then swarm out into the water column in search of a host. The full life cycle is completed in about two weeks.

One of the first signs of velvet is the infected fish rubbing against hard objects in an attempt to rid itself of the parasite. Fins will become clamped, breathing labored and fast because of gill infestation, and activity levels and appetite will decrease. In a darkened room with the tank lights off and the aid of a flashlight it is possible to see a gold-, rust-, or even gray- or white-colored dust on the fins or body of the fish. Later, in advanced stages of the disease, it may be possible to see small white pustules and the skin may become grayish and slough off.

Treatment for Velvet

Like ich, *Piscinoodinium* is targeted during the free-swimming stage of its life cycle. The organism contains chlorophyll and must photosynthesize to survive. Keeping the tank as close to completely dark as possible will cause extreme stress for the parasite and slow its life cycle. Increasing the water temperature to 82°F (27°C) speeds up the life cycle and shortens the treatment period, but also will more rapidly increase the number of dinospores. Even with increased aeration, the infected loaches may be further stressed and mortality may increase.

Since velvet is frequently misdiagnosed until the infestation has progressed to a dangerous level, it would be better to maintain the current tank temperature, or possibly lower it slightly. If lowering the temperature, be certain that it remains within a range the fish will tolerate. Lowering the temperature will slow reproduction of the parasite and will also significantly extend the length of treatment. Lower temperatures in the 59° to 63°F (15° to 17°C) range will reduce mortality rates, but development of the dinospores may take 11 days or more. While temperatures this low would be acceptable for weather loaches, balitorids, and some *Sinibotia* species, tropical loaches could not tolerate these temperatures.

Aquarium salt may be added to ease the fishes' breathing due to gill damage caused by the parasite. One teaspoon per 5 gallons (19 liters) is often recommended, but loaches do not always tolerate salt well. Be sure to observe your fishes closely. If the addition of salt causes further stress as evidenced by the inhabitants' behavior, do a large water change to reduce the salinity and continue treatment without the salt.

Thorough vacuuming of the substrate combined with large water changes should eventually decontaminate the tank. Be sure to replace medication lost in water changes during treatment. It is extremely important to be observant of any signs of re-infection and to continue treatment for several days after all signs of velvet are gone.

> *The best treatment for Piscinoodinium is prevention. All new fishes should be quarantined to prevent introduction of the parasite to the community tank. Maintaining high water quality at all times reduces the risk of infection. Offering fishes a healthy balanced diet will also increase their resistance to such parasites.*

Hillstream Loach Diseases

The sucker-bodied members of the family Balitoridae, while theoretically being at risk from all diseases, have been noted by the specialists in their care as being blissfully free of most of the aforementioned conditions. There is one problem, though, that seems peculiar to these species. The symptoms include patchy loss of color and body markings, reduced appetite, and, often, increased respiration. It has been noted that this condition also seems to affect the suction capabilities of the fishes. The adaptations that allow them to stick to smooth surfaces are compromised, probably due to muscle weakness. Instead of staying put, stuck to the glass, an affected fish will gradually slip down the surface. The symptoms are sometimes seen in newly imported fishes, no doubt from the stresses involved in capture and transport. Once these symptoms are noted, death is usually very swift. The exact cause is presently unknown. Sometimes a fish can seem healthy and feeding one minute, only to be dead in a few hours. Close observation is required, particularly with new fishes.

Prevention

Loaches are stressed by a number of factors. Stress negatively affects their immune systems. Capture and shipping create an enormous amount of stress for these fishes, which is why many new arrivals to the aquarium shop and to the home tank quickly show signs of disease. Quarantining new fishes, especially wild-caught fishes like loaches, is one of the best preventive measures that can be undertaken in aquarium practice. Medical treatment may be an initial necessity for a large proportion of loaches, and many keepers treat for internal parasites as a prophylactic rule when quarantining new fishes.

Once through the quarantine period the best way to reduce the likelihood that any of these diseases will manifest is through prevention. Experienced keepers of loaches know that there is no substitute for personal observation. Keeping a watchful eye on the tank inhabitants and their environment, performing weekly water changes, and monitoring water parameters is the best way to prevent disease outbreaks in the aquarium.

Situations Leading to Stress
- Overcrowding
- Poor water quality
- Inadequate water changes
- Breakdown of a well-established biological filter, or a poorly established biological filter, leading to nitrites or ammonia in the water column
- Inadequate oxygen
- Slow water movement
- Excess food left in the tank
- Transportation and introduction into the home aquarium, including rough handling and netting
- Sudden temperature changes

How to Reduce Stress
The water must be kept clean. Regular weekly water changes are recommended along with general tank maintenance like cleaning the inside walls of the tank and vacuuming the substrate.

All spoiled food must be removed from the aquarium quickly. Vegetable matter, both food items and dead plant leaves, should be removed before they can decay in the warm water.

Each loach must have enough room and shaded hiding places for it to feel safe. They should be kept in small groups of their own kind and never with aggressive tankmates that will harass them.

Loaches should not be placed in aquaria that are exposed to noise or in very busy areas of the home. The fish should have time to "be by themselves," when they can rest or otherwise behave as they would in nature. Their surroundings should not be constantly changing or disturbed.

In nature loaches benefit from a varied diet of crustaceans, invertebrates, and plant matter. It is important to provide captive loaches with a similar varied menu. It is likely imperative to the maintenance of their immune systems and for the benefit of their general health and well-being.

Chapter 7

The Family
Botiidae

The family Cobitidae was divided into two subfamilies: Botiinae and Cobitinae. In February 2007 a revision was made, reorganizing families based on nuclear genetic data. Botiine loaches were assigned to their own family, Botiidae, and comprise some of the most popular and available aquarium fishes, but there are some remarkable and highly sought after cobitid loaches as well, including the kuhli loaches, the horseface loach, and others (see Chapter 8 for these loaches). All members of the revised family Cobitidae have suborbital spines. Although the taxonomy can be confusing, it is helpful to understand how these fishes are classified in order to better appreciate how closely certain species are related.

Subfamily Botiidae

Until changes in the taxonomy in 2004, the subfamily Botiinae contained only three genera: *Botia, Leptobotia,* and *Parabotia*. The genus Botia was broken up into more specific groups (these are discussed in the following pages). This family encompasses a group of fishes that are rich in diversity. They can range in size from the enormous clown loach (*Chromobotia macracanthus*), 12 inches (30.5 cm) in length, to the diminutive dwarf loach (*Yasuhikotakia sidthimunki*), which reaches only 2.25 inches (5.5 cm). Likewise, botiid loaches come in all shapes and hues. The various species sport a great variety of body markings, and many species bear a spectrum of attractive colors on their flanks or fins. This whole group of loaches has now been reclassified into the family Botiidae.

Botiid Taxonomy

The family Botiidae is relatively small. At present it has only 33 recognized distinct species, but it is growing all the time. Recently three or four new species have been discovered, most notably the angelicus botia (*Botia kubotai*), which has been enthusiastically received within the hobby.

Because of various differences in physiology among the loaches, in 2004 a proposed change to the genus *Botia* separated the various species into

A sleeping clown loach.

The exact source of the "clicking" sounds made by *Yasuhikotakia modesta* is subject to further research, but testing has shown that this loach produces high-intensity broadband knocking sounds or clicks, with no harmonic structure, with peak energy of 469 Hz.

five newly assigned genera. These genera contain just about all the botiid loaches that are either desirable or available to the aquarist. Only these fishes will be covered in detail in this book.

1. The clown loach, long considered to be within the genus *Botia*, is currently thought to have characteristics unique enough to justify its own genus, *Chromobotia*. Its new designation is *Chromobotia macracanthus*.

2. The so-called "true" *Botia* species remain in a new and smaller version of the genus *Botia*.

3. Loaches of the *"hymenophysa* complex" are now designated as being within the genus *Syncrossus*.

4. The species of the *"modesta* complex" of loaches falls into the new genus *Yasuhikotakia*.

5. *Sinibotia* is a genus covering a number of species that are found primarily in China.

These changes are quite recent, and because most resources, both in the literature and on the Internet, still refer to all of these fishes under the genus *Botia*, a certain amount of cross-referencing may be necessary. Individual changes in taxonomy and synonyms for the different species will be covered in the species descriptions.

Botiidae Characteristics

Every member of the family possesses a distinctive suborbital spine situated between the eye and the mouth. This sharp spine is extendable and is kept hidden in a pouch when not in use. The spine can be employed as a weapon when one loach spars with another, or it can be used as a defense mechanism to discourage potential predators. Some botiid loaches have been found lodged in the throats of dead birds in their natural environment.

Another intriguing physical characteristic of the family is the ability of its members to produce "clicking" noises. These noises are generated during feeding or during territorial disputes. One theory behind this behavior is that the clicking is produced by the rubbing of muscles against each other in the body of the fish. Another theory says that it comes from the rasping of pharyngeal "teeth" in the throat. Still another theory is that the sound is produced through a simple sharp intake of food or water—that the noise is actually the result of suction.

All botiids use noise production as a means of deferring actual combat over food or cover. Many fishes produce "honest" sounds that can be interpreted by members of the same species as a way of determining dominance and physical fitness. In other words, the sound informs each fish of the likely strengths of another fish and the possibility of defeating it. A study on *Yasuhikotakia morleti* showed that its short-duration broadband clicks were used in territorial disputes as a way of avoiding escalations of combat with superior competitors.

One factor that has been studied carefully is how botiid species perceive noise. They are regarded as hearing specialists.

All members of the family Cobitidae and Botiidae have reduced swim bladders due to their bottom-living tendencies, but the organ is modified in various ways. In botiid species it has been shown that reduction of the swim bladder actually increases hearing sensitivity.

In all species the anterior part of the swim bladder is encapsulated in bone to varying degrees. In *Y. modesta*, there is cranial encapsulation of this anterior part, which should reduce hearing capacity. In this species and other botiids there are adaptations that counter this effect. The inner ear is connected to gas-filled cavities that transmit the pressure variations of sounds through a series of ossicles known as the Weberian ossicles. The anterior part of the swim bladder is often called the camera aerea Weberian (CAW) apparatus. This name indicates its importance to the hearing via the Weberian apparatus and the assumption that it no longer performs a hydrostatic function as in free-swimming fishes.

In botiid species there are openings within the bony encapsulation that open into muscle-free chambers filled with lymph. These connect to oval windows under the skin of the fish at the lateral line level in the area of the trunk that is devoid of musculature approximately in line with the pectoral fins. These chambers help to transmit sound pressure waves from the water, via the CAW to the Weberian apparatus and on to the inner ear. It has been proven that this improves the hearing capacity of the fish throughout its full hearing range. It is assumed that the combination of these apparatuses may also work in reverse to amplify and transmit

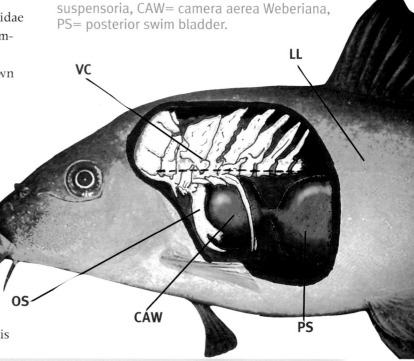

Schematic showing swim bladder encapsulation. VC= vertebral column, LL= lateral line, OS= ossa suspensoria, CAW= camera aerea Weberiana, PS= posterior swim bladder.

sounds produced by the fish out to the water surrounding the fish.

Species in the genus *Leptobotia* have increased bony encapsulation of the CAW compared to botiids but still have lateral openings connecting to muscle-free sinus, so it must be assumed that their hearing is also augmented.

All botiid species have very tiny scales, which makes them susceptible to impurities in the water and more sensitive to many medications. Full explanation of precautions to be taken when medicating are given in Chapter 6.

The geographical distribution of botiid loaches is as diverse as the range of their physical appearance. The majority of them can be found in the fresh waters of southern Asia, in countries ranging from India to Indonesia. Some species such as *Sinibotia robusta* can be found as far north as central China, while *Botia almorhae* can be found as far west as Pakistan.

Sinibotia robusta. Found in parts of China and Vietnam.

Care of Botiid Loaches

Like the majority of bottom-dwelling species of tropical fishes, members of the family Botiidae must be provided with sheltered hiding spots. Caves, crevices, and stacked wood or stones are preferable (see Chapter 3). For smaller species such as *Yasuhikotakia sidthimunki*, broadleaf plants like Amazon swords can provide suitable shelter.

Sand or rounded fine gravel substrates are good choices, since botiids are digging fishes. As mentioned previously, precautions should be taken so that sharp-edged rocks and surfaces that may injure their delicate barbels are not included in the tank.

Another factor to take into account for a botiid aquarium is the strength of lighting provided. Many such loaches are sensitive to bright light and may keep to the caves until lights are turned off for the night. In order to increase the activity of botiids during the day, subdued lighting is preferable. This type of lighting can be achieved either by lowering the bulb/tube intensity or by

the addition of floating plants. The use of fast-growing tall plants like *Ludwigia* can create areas of greater shade in the aquarium, which will appeal to these loaches.

It is also possible to light only one end of an aquarium. Tanks lighted by bulbs are simple enough to modify for this effect, and tanks lighted by fluorescent tubes can be fitted with shorter lights: a 24-inch (60-cm) tube can be incorporated on a 48-inch (120-cm) tank. This method provides half of the tank with at least subdued lighting. Some keepers have found that lighting a tank this way encourages loaches to spend more time swimming about the whole area of the aquarium.

Most loaches, botiids in particular, observe the reactions of other fishes in nature and use their activity levels as an indicator of safety. The relaxed behavior of schooling fishes signals the absence of predators. For this reason, loaches will be more active if housed with a small group of schooling species such as barbs or danios. When used for this purpose, these species are known as "dither fishes." Their strong instinct for schooling and their high activity levels will make the loaches bolder and more active for a greater part of the day. If housed alone in an aquarium, a group of botiid loaches will interpret the absence of these fishes as a possible indication of danger and will not wish to leave the security of rockwork or other hiding places.

Dither fishes must be chosen to suit the species of loach being kept. Certain botiids can be somewhat

Yasuhikotakia morleti. It is important to offer loaches more hiding spots than there are fishes in the tank because having an abundance of hiding spots can serve to reduce the sometimes aggressive or territorial behavior of the loaches.

Botia rostrata.

aggressive and therefore should have robust tankmates. White Cloud Mountain minnows, for instance, would not be a good mix with large species of *Syncrossus*, who might view them as food, but they would be perfectly at home with smaller *Botia* species.

Tank size is crucial for housing either a single group of one species or multiple species. *Botia*, *Chromobotia*, and some other species are gregarious and must be kept in groups in order to ensure their well-being. The size of the tank greatly depends on which species is desired by the aquarist. A small group of *Yasuhikotakia sidthimunki* can be successfully housed in a 10- or 20-gallon (38- or 76-liter) tank. A larger group of these small loaches will need a bigger tank to thrive. The more area

loaches have to school, the healthier they will be. Small tanks are to be avoided for almost all species of a medium or larger size. One should think of the deep streams in which they live and plan to provide reasonable room for all botiid species in the aquarium. Here the true rule is "the bigger, the better."

Botiid species should be kept in groups of no less than three of any given species. Plenty of swimming space should be provided, because these fishes generally explore their surroundings in a tight group, usually occupying the middle and lower strata of the aquarium. Additionally, any aquarium housing botiids should have a secure cover, since many species of the group are superb jumpers. Perhaps the best jumper is *Botia kubotai*,

It's All in the Name

The name clown loach suits *Chromobotia macracanthus* for a number of reasons. Its garish colors are rare in freshwater fishes, but its behavior in the tank is one of the main reasons it is so endearing to loach keepers. Clown loaches tend to rest on their sides, or even upside down on the floor of the tank or in caves. Discovery of a fish in this position can be genuinely shocking to new aquarists, who immediately assume that the fish lying prone on the tank floor must be dead. After the first or second time this trait is witnessed by the aquarist the automatic panic reaction tends to subside. With clown loaches patience is a virtue. Very often they will suddenly wake from their inverted torpor and dart off to a safe dark spot in the tank.

While no one is certain why they behave this way, it often manages to stir the loach keeper into a frenzy of concern. It is usually better to wait and see what the loach chooses to do rather than panic and assume the worst.

Another behavioral characteristic of most members of the genera *Botia* and *Chromobotia* is the tendency to explore the aquarium in groups, briskly swimming to the upper stratum of the aquarium only to speedily zoom back down to the bottom. This routine swimming pattern, commonly referred to as "the loachy dance," can be repeated for hours on end. It is particularly noticeable when several *Botia* are introduced to a new home, or even minor changes to the setup of an established tank are made. Under these circumstances, some individuals may swim about rapidly in a repetitive pattern, displaying their distress. It is advisable during cleaning of a botiid tank to return any large items of décor to their original positions. The relief of familiar shelter is evident in the loaches' behavior.

The Clown Loach

Chances are good that most loach collections began with the arrival of a small group of clown loaches. They are the most widely available and popular loach in the hobby and arguably the most brightly colored of all loach species. Because of this, they have been prized additions to the tropical aquarium for many years, and they are the single most documented and discussed loach in the literature, including reference books and resources on the Internet.

Harvesting Clown Loaches

Chromobotia macracanthus is harvested from jungle streams on a couple of islands in Indonesia. The clown's love of hiding in tight places is utilized

which can leap out of a tank with the water level as low as 4 inches (10 cm) below the top.

Botiids can squeeze themselves through even the tightest of spaces. Since many of these loaches inhabit flowing waters, they may seek out a source of water movement in the aquarium, such as that of a filter or airstone. It is not uncommon for them to be found in the various tubes and boxes of a filtration system, gleefully swimming in the turbulence of the churning water. Tactics to avoid these occurrences are discussed in Chapter 2.

Botiid behavior in the home aquarium is frequently eye-catching and can be startling. Some of these loaches consistently rest upside down, under décor, or on their sides, as if they were dead.

A school of clown loaches in the middle of what some hobbyists refer to as "the loachy dance."

Chromobotia macracanthus
(Bleeker, 1852)

Synonyms: *Botia macracanthus, Botia macracantha, Cobitis macracantha*

Common Names: clown loach, striped mouse-fish (China)

Distribution: Borneo and Sumatra. May exist on other islands

Occurrences: Kalimantan Tengah, Borneo, Indonesia
Kalimantan Timur, Borneo, Indonesia
Barito River Basin, Sungei Bari, Borneo, Indonesia
Sungai Lalah, Indragiri, Sumatra, Indonesia
Palembang River, Sumatra, Indonesia
Sungai Paku, Indonesia
Kulai, Malaysia

Habitat: inland freshwater streams; sand, pebbles, boulders; leaf litter, fallen trees

Ideal Tank Parameters: pH 6.5 to 7; Temp 78° to 83°F (25° to 30°C)

they reach a significant size and age. For this reason, the government of Indonesia forbids the export of clown loaches over 6 inches (15 cm). Such large specimens are not as desired by the Western aquarium trade, so small, immature fish are preferred by the people who collect them in the wild. It is estimated that as many as 20 million immature clowns are exported from Borneo and Sumatra each year. Large catches in the wild can be seasonal. The catch is often housed in large ponds and cared for so that a more even distribution of the fish may be exported to the trade throughout the year.

The seasonal nature of the trade can result in fluctuating retail prices for the fish. The potential owner may find that the species is quite expensive, but later in the year fish of the same size are much cheaper. There has been an increase in the

The *tabung* is lifted from the water and emptied into buckets. *Chromobotia macracanthus* collection site near Jambi, Sumatra, Indonesia.

as a means of capture. Bamboo tubes called *tabung* are placed into the streams and left for a while; then the ends of the tubes are capped and the tubes are removed with the fish trapped inside. Entrance holes in the bamboo poles are cut to size so that the collector can regulate the size of each fish caught. In Borneo, these poles are bundled together, but in Sumatra the *tabung* are laid individually.

It seems that these loaches do not reproduce until

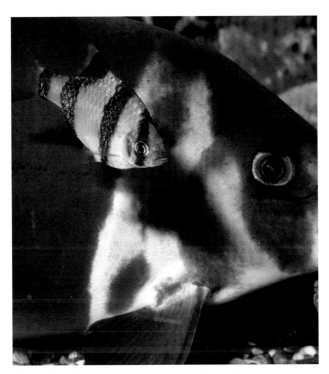

Clown loaches can grow to lengths of over 12 inches (30.5 cm). Just look how this clown dwarfs its barb tankmate.

grow so should their environment, but even small specimens should be given ample room. They should not be housed in a tank under 20 gallons (76 liters) in volume, even as immature individuals. The clown loaches that introduce the Preface and Afterword of this book are shown at actual size, and give an impression of just how large the species can grow over time.

Water Conditions

Like other loaches, clowns require water conditions that resemble the flowing streams where they are captured. Their water must be kept clean through regular large water changes (30 to 50 percent once a week). They prefer soft, slightly acidic water but can tolerate a fairly wide range of pH as long as water parameters don't suddenly change. These fish have tiny scales and they are exceptionally sensitive to the presence of ammonia and nitrites in their water, so they should only be added to an aquarium with a fully established biological filter.

availability of very small clowns, attributed to artificial breeding in large ponds in Thailand using hormonal injections. Researchers in Florida are perfecting a hormone breeding protocol for these fish for use by Florida fish farms.

Biggest of Them All

Clowns really are the giants among loaches. A mature clown can exceed a foot in length (30.5 cm), but it may take as long as 20 years to reach this size. They are best suited for aquarists who are able commit to many years of care and can provide for their large size with a tank of 90 gallons (340 liters) or more. As clown loaches

Clowns are known to live for over 40 years, so the possibility exists for having to make provision for them in one's will!

Markings and Coloration

C. macracanthus is a moderately elongated, laterally compressed loach, with an arched back and a fairly flat belly. Its body is a rich orange-gold color with three wide black stripes across the head, back, and rear of the dorsal fin. Variation occurs frequently in the shape of the stripes. Sometimes the dark band does not extend to the belly and can give the appearance of a saddle behind the dorsal fin. Sometimes the stripes may appear like pieces of a jigsaw in shape. Some enthusiasts actually make a point of collecting clown loaches with unusual markings. Often in mature adults the dark bands will become bisected with thin silver bands and the outer edges of each stripe may develop a paler outline.

Due to regionally separated breeding groups, their isolation has led to distinct differences, which may not be particularly noticeable until two fish from different areas are placed beside one another.

A quick identification of origin can be made by the color of the pelvic fins. Fish from Borneo have a black area in the base and center of the fin, and usually the front (hard) ray is red-orange with the end of the fin being clear, smoky, or slightly red. In clown loaches from Sumatra the pelvic fin is all red-orange.

There are other geographical differences that can be observed. The dorsal and anal fins have less yellow at their lead edges in Sumatran fish. The rear stripe extends onto the caudal peduncle in clowns from Borneo, but not in Sumatran fish. Sumatran clowns tend to have some redness in the caudal fin, extending onto the caudal peduncle.

Clowns from Kalimantan, on the island of Borneo, are basically like the ones found on Sumatra but have a more intense red coloration and are the most desirable for the aquarist. Fish from Sumatra are reported as sometimes having a silver sheen to the body. This is not seen in specimens from Kalimantan.

The clown loach on the left is "grayed out."

Clowns are able to change their coloration at times. These changes can be based on mood, aggression, stress, or other factors. Often an aquarist new to keeping clowns will be alarmed by suddenly finding that one or more fish have lost most of their normal coloration and become very light and faded. This phenomenon is now almost universally referred to as "graying out."

Clown loaches have a social hierarchy, and every so often a dispute may develop over food or determination of dominance within the group. At this time violent sparring matches may occur. If two fish are engaged in such trials of strength, it is common for them to "gray out" and assume a distinctive body posture. The fish will adopt a bold, tail-down attitude with fins spread. They may go up against one another and shove bodily or slash with their tails. Their opponents in these battles may darken. The differences in lighter and darker fading have to do with dominance, and one fish in the group—the alpha loach, may exhibit this phenomenon more regularly than the others. It is also common to see one fish from a group grow more rapidly than the others.

Clown loaches can "gray out" quickly, particularly at feeding time. Depending on the lighting this color change may show a kind of greenish metallic sheen across the whole body and is most noticeable over the stripes. The edges of the stripes tend to have a paler area than the rest of the stripe at this time.

Defense Mechanism

Clowns have thick lips surrounded by four pairs of barbels, which are larger above the mouth. Halfway between their eyes and mouth there is a sharp retractable spine, used in defense. This effective device, which has skewered a few loach keepers over the years, rarely appears and is

What's That Noise?
Often during mealtimes, or during territorial spats, clowns produce a surprisingly loud clicking noise. This noise occurs with some of the other botiid species but is very common in *C. macracanthus* and can surprise aquarists who are new to the species. Dominant (alpha) fish are often the most vocal and will warn others away from a particular tasty morsel with a loud click. The whole group may make clicking noises.

normally retracted within a narrow pouch beneath the skin. All keepers of clown and other botiid loaches should be aware of this defensive mechanism. A quick puncture wound from a clown loach is not a good experience in any situation. The wound, although small, is very painful; it often is deep and will bleed profusely. The suborbital spine is sometimes extended during transport when the loach is distressed by being caught in a net. Because of this, care should be taken when the fish are emptied from nets so that they do not become painfully entangled. Also, this fearsome weaponry can make short work of plastic transport bags, so these bags must be multi-layered for security. Clowns are peaceful loaches, however, and most aquarists will never actually see a clown loach's suborbital spine. The spines may be raised during sparring between clowns, but generally this only results in scratches on the other fish's flanks. Scratches will heal quickly in healthy fish.

Protect Your Clowns

Clown loaches are notoriously prone to ich and often bring this protozoan infection into their new homes. They are also perhaps the loach most commonly affected by "skinny disease." (See Chapter 6 for a review of these diseases.) They are among the most inquisitive species and will sometimes explore hiding spots and openings in the tank that are easier to enter than exit. (See Chapter 2 for more information on safe tank setups for overly adventuresome loaches.)

Eating Habits

At times clown loaches can be fussy eaters, rejecting food that is coveted by other loach species. Flake food is often ignored, but it can be integrated into their diet over time. Frozen foods such as bloodworms, daphnia, and brine shrimp are usually well received. Larger individuals are fond of krill or chopped shrimp. Clowns will relish fresh vegetables, such as cucumber suitably weighted to keep it on the bottom of the tank. They will eat sinking algae wafers and enjoy sinking pellets formulated for carnivorous fishes. Some live foods can be used if they are available from a known clean source. Chopped or small whole earthworms will be avidly eaten.

Clown loaches do better in groups than when they are kept individually. Remember that adult clowns are large fish, so make sure your tank is large enough to accommodate the future growth of the entire school.

The More the Merrier

This species should only be kept in numbers of three or more. Because of their sophisticated social interactions with other clowns (and other loaches), keeping them individually does not satisfy their need for socialization and will adversely affect their physical health. In pairs, they can become territorial and standoffish, but with three or more in the tank, their true highly social nature becomes apparent.

There are few sights more appealing to any aquarist than a group of *C. macracanthus* schooling through the tank near the glass. In high arcs, up near the surface and down through the lower levels, they will swim in unison, in perfect formation. It is no wonder that this loach is highly sought after and worth understanding. If kept in the right environment, the clown loach will thrive for decades, proving to be one of the most interesting, beautiful, and engaging fish to inhabit a freshwater tank.

> **Did You Know?**
> Botia almorhae *was once thought to be distinct from* B. lohachata, *but the two species have since been combined.*

Genus *Botia*

"True" *Botia* species have four pairs of barbels. They are generally more compact than other loaches in body shape and have arched backs and forked caudal fins. This genus contains the following species: *B. almorhae, B. dario, B. histrionica, B. kubotai, B. rostrata,* and *B. striata.* These six species, along with the clown loach, may be among the most popular loaches in the hobby; if not for their attractive colors and markings then for their generally placid dispositions. Squabbles and fights rarely take place among this group, and different species tend to interact with one another to some extent and school together.

Botia almorhae

Botia almorhae is dubbed the yoyo loach for the juvenile fish's distinctive markings. Small round patches that appear mid-flank separate two to three "Y"-shaped vertical stripes forming what looks to be the word "yoyo"

You will witness some very interesting behavior in schools of clown loaches.

Botia almorhae
(Gray, 1831)

Synonyms: *Botia lohachata*

Common Names: yoyo loach, almorha loach, Pakistani loach, reticulate loach, baghae (Nepali), jabo (Hindi), bou mach (Bengali)

Distribution: Pakistan, India, Nepal, Bangladesh

Occurrences: Almorha Hills, India
Garhwal Himalayas, India
Tista River, Darjeeling, India
Chambal River, Rajasthan, India
Sone River, Uttar Pradesh, India
Kathmandu, Nepal
Jamuna River, Bangladesh

Habitat: streams that feed sections of the Ganges River system, the Jamuna River, and others. Juveniles are found in lower sections, while it seems adults migrate upstream to higher altitudes. Does not occur in elevations below 620 feet (189 meters). Rocky or gravel substrate preferred to sand

Ideal Tank Parameters: pH 6.6 to 7.2; Temp, 76° to 82°F (22° to 27.7°C)

Hiding spots in the tank are essential, as they are with all other loaches. Piled rocks or tangles of driftwood are suitable, since this fish is found in pool areas of highland streams. As with other loaches, clean water is a top priority, so frequent water changes must be undertaken. *B. almorhae* seems uninterested in plants and is therefore a good candidate for the planted loach tank.

This robust loach reaches an adult size of 6.8 inches (17 cm). *B. almorhae* is active both day and night and should be provided with a fair amount of swimming room on the floor of the tank. Individuals will frequently rest on top of tank décor or wedge themselves into tight crevices and caves.

Botia almorhae, the "yoyo" loach.

on the sides of the fish. These markings are a chocolate brown to dark-charcoal over the silvery-gray body of the fish. *B. almorhae* is a peaceful loach and is perhaps more active than other *Botia* species, but certainly not more aggressive. It combines well with other *Botia* species but should be kept in small groups of no less than three in either a community or species tank.

Botia almorhae hiding under bogwood. Are my fish dead? New loach keepers must grow accustomed to seeing their fish resting sideways on the bottom of the tank or beneath decor like these yoyo loaches.

Unusual among *Botia* species, *B. almorhae* shows sexual dimorphism—that is, sexing the fish is a more simple undertaking. Females have a distinctly longer snout than males and have a more rounded belly. Males, in maturity, can develop reddish highlights around the barbels and mouth and at the margins of the pectoral fins. Males may have a darker body coloring, making their "Y" markings less obvious.

The "Y" markings are also more clearly defined in juveniles of both sexes and can fade or become crosshatched in adulthood, forming a reticulated pattern. Like many other *Botia*, during any fighting between individuals over dominance within the group this species will "gray out." With the contrast between the body and markings reduced the fish may appear either quite dark gray or a light silver-gold.

Some adults of this species closely resemble *B. histrionica, B. rostrata,* and in some instances *B. kubotai.* All of these species are thought to be closely related. Positive identification of immature specimens of any of these species can be challenging.

Botia almorhae has not been bred in the aquarium, but they have been bred in pools on commercial farms in Southeast Asia. The eggs are bright green, and both the eggs and fry are buoyant.

Botia dario
(Hamilton, 1822)

Synonyms: *Cobitis dario, Cobitis geto, Diacantha flavicauda*

Common Names: Bengal loach, queen loach, necktie loach (vernacular use in India), bou mach (Bengali), botuk mach (Assamese), leiterschmerle (German)

Distribution: India, Bangladesh, Bhutan

Occurrences: Ganges River, India
Palashwari, India
Jove River, India
Jumna River, Bangladesh
Gaylephug River, Bhutan

Habitat: slower moving but clear mountain streams found in foothills to high mountain tropical regions south of the Himalayas. Also found in wide rivers and their tributaries

Ideal Tank Parameters: pH 6.5 to 7.5; Temp 72° to 79°F (23° to 26°C)

Botia dario

This elegant-looking *Botia* can grow to 6 inches (15.2 cm) but will likely not achieve that size in the aquarium. They are very social creatures and should be kept in groups of at least three. They make excellent companions for other gentle *Botia* loaches. Inquisitive and quick-witted, Bengal loaches will explore in packs and will show brief but persuasive bursts of aggression over food and hiding spots, often accompanied by vigorous clicking sounds. These skirmishes will not cause damage to other fishes but instead just reveal their headstrong attitude in the community setting.

One of the less picky eaters, *Botia dario* will accept flake food, frozen foods such as bloodworms and brine shrimp, sinking algae or carnivore pellets or wafers, and fresh vegetables. Raw seedless cucumber is a favorite. Care should be given not to overfeed. These fish will not know when to stop and will respond to an overabundance of food with an overabundance of waste.

They must be provided with numerous hiding spots on the aquarium floor, but they are by no means a retiring species. They are one of the most active of the genus and quick to systematically dismantle certain species of aquarium plants by

Botia dario.

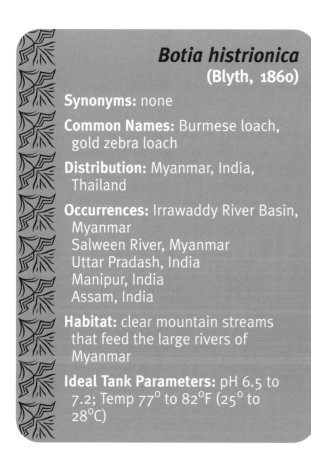

Botia histrionica
(Blyth, 1860)

Synonyms: none

Common Names: Burmese loach, gold zebra loach

Distribution: Myanmar, India, Thailand

Occurrences: Irrawaddy River Basin, Myanmar
Salween River, Myanmar
Uttar Pradash, India
Manipur, India
Assam, India

Habitat: clear mountain streams that feed the large rivers of Myanmar

Ideal Tank Parameters: pH 6.5 to 7.2; Temp 77° to 82°F (25° to 28°C)

scraps with other fish. Four pairs of barbels surround the down-turned mouth. The dorsal fin appears centrally, directly above the anal fins. Like clown loaches, *B. dario* individuals have large heads, but they are notable for having a pronounced convex curvature from the forehead to snout.

During times of subdued lighting, at dawn or dusk, *Botia dario* can sometimes be seen swimming in formation in long slow arcs throughout the aquarium, occasionally coming to a full stop and falling slowly to the substrate as a group.

Botia histrionica

Botia histrionica is a gentle and gregarious loach, well suited to the community aquarium. No two specimens bear the same markings. Young fish have an obvious metallic golden sheen to their skin that fades as they mature, becoming more silvery-gray in most specimens. Sometimes the golden color remains into maturity, possibly due to diet. Mature specimens reach a size of 5.2 inches (13 cm). Vertical black

plucking and discarding leaves. Plants such as broadleaf *Echinodorus* species and Java fern are a better choice for these loaches.

More dorsally compressed than *Chromobotia macracanthus*, the Bengal loach's body is a pale metallic yellow, bisected along its length by seven to ten vertical stripes, which are a rich chocolate brown. Like many other loach species, it is prone to "graying out" when agitated. The whole skin will become a pale, ashen gray color during occasional

Botia histrionica.

bands extend right to the belly and may extend onto the pelvic and anal fins. The dorsal and caudal fins of this species bear a distinctive black dot or ellipse. A black line that crosses the eye branches off and extends toward the mouth. The marking on the dorsal fin is one helpful way of distinguishing juveniles of this species from young *B. kubotai, B. rostrata,* and *B. almorhae.*

Loaches

This is one of the least shy of all the *Botia* species. It is still important to provide *B. histrionica* with plenty of sheltered hiding spots, but generally they spend more time in the open resting on tank décor or rooting through the substrate in a constant search for food. It is possible that they are less sensitive to light levels than others in the genus. Fine gravel is the best substrate for these loaches, but sand will also do well. They mix very well with similar species such as *B. almorhae* and *B. kubotai* and may interact with them as with their own kind.

B. histrionica is inquisitive and playful and will chase or "corral" other bottom-dwelling fishes for hours without the slightest sign of aggression. They are also one of the easiest species to feed. They will readily accept flake food, frozen invertebrates, vegetables, and freeze-dried offerings. They sometimes graze plants but are less likely to do so if their diet is supplemented with vegetables like blanched spinach or cucumber. Boiled peas, removed from their outer skins, also are a favorite item.

Botia histrionica.

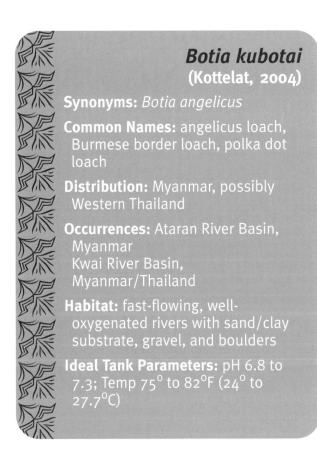

Botia kubotai
(Kottelat, 2004)

Synonyms: *Botia angelicus*

Common Names: angelicus loach, Burmese border loach, polka dot loach

Distribution: Myanmar, possibly Western Thailand

Occurrences: Ataran River Basin, Myanmar
Kwai River Basin, Myanmar/Thailand

Habitat: fast-flowing, well-oxygenated rivers with sand/clay substrate, gravel, and boulders

Ideal Tank Parameters: pH 6.8 to 7.3; Temp 75° to 82°F (24° to 27.7°C)

Botia kubotai

This *Botia* was discovered quite recently. Its beautiful markings and docile nature have quickly made it one of the most popular loaches available. It makes an excellent candidate for the community tank and mixes well with other gentle loaches.

The juvenile *Botia kubotai* has several large ivory- or gold-colored oval markings on its body, usually eight per side, with four to five black bands separating them. The upper and lower sets of four stripes are divided by a horizontal black lateral bar that runs from behind the eye to the caudal peduncle. The markings on this loach may change dramatically as the fish matures. Juvenile specimens of this species are extremely similar to those of *B. almorhae, B. histrionica,* and *B. rostrata.*

There are two distinctive types noted in the coloration of this species. There is the "normal" type, mentioned above, and also the "melanistic" (i.e., black) type. Melanistic specimens have proportionately more black on the body. Within the black areas, at the crossing points of the lateral and

Yasuhikotakia sidthimunki (right) are peaceful loaches and they mix well with *Botia* species such as this *B. kubotai* (left).

vertical stripes, there are small ivory dots, which sometimes have a bluish sheen, enhancing the splendor of this species. Generally, for a given size of fish, the melanistic form has more of these dots. As the fish matures the large oval spots break up into smaller, rounder white areas on a black body. These changes happen with both types. The head of *B. kubotai* bears a striking resemblance to that of *B. almorhae*. Pattern variations are frequent among individuals of this species, even within each type, and each individual seems to bear slightly different markings.

B. kubotai should be provided with plenty of swimming room. It is a very active species that can grow to 6 inches (15 cm) when kept in a well-suited aquarium. A group of three or more *B. kubotai* is appropriate, as these fish have complex social interactions. Periodically they will swim head-to-tail with one another at astonishing speed in a tight circle. Similar to other species of *Botia*, during these interactions the fish may gray out. When this occurs, they bear a striking resemblance to older, mature *B. almorhae*. The contrast between the black and ivory completely changes to shades of gray. The purpose of this behavior is not clear, but it may have to do with establishing dominance or territory. It may also be some sort of mating ritual, but these fish have not been bred in the tank setting to date. *B. kubotai* has also been

observed performing this lightning-fast circular dance with *B. histrionica* that shared the same tank. The two species are not dissimilar in basic coloration or shape.

Plants, wood, and rocky caves should be provided to offer *B. kubotai* many choices of shelter. Multiple shelter options will increase their sense of security, which will generally make the fish bolder. Combining them with other loaches or suitable dither fishes will also increase their activity.

Current is recommended for this species, to better simulate its natural habitat and to increase oxygenation of the water. *B. kubotai* responds well to the addition of a powerhead to its tank for this purpose. Particularly when first introduced to a new tank, *B. kubotai* will often swim against a current as if trying to swim "upstream." They may swim into powerhead outlets or up the ramp of a hang-on-the-back filter. This behavior will diminish once the fish are settled into their new home. *B. kubotai* enjoys digging and even burrowing if a soft substrate of sand or fine gravel is provided.

As with all the other *Botia* species, bloodworms are a favorite food item, but *B. kubotai* will also accept freeze-dried and fresh foods as well as quality brands of flake and pellet food. They have also been observed grazing on plants and will nibble at cucumber.

> **Botia kubotai,** *like other scaleless or small-scaled fish, is susceptible to ich and other skin parasites. Signs of illness warrant immediate quarantine and treatment.*

Botia rostrata

Botia rostrata is closely related to *B. histrionica, B. almorhae,* and *B. kubotai*; this is most evident when correct identification of juvenile specimens is attempted. Like these other loaches, *B. rostrata* has a mainly cream to golden color crossed by variable vertical bands of black. This species is distinct because of the pattern of the black bands, which appear two at a time. The bands can zigzag or curve and can be punctuated by silvery circular markings (similar to *B. kubotai*) as the fish matures.

This gentle loach grows to an adult size of 3.33 inches (8.5 cm). It is an excellent choice for the community loach tank if kept in numbers of three or more and generally behaves like other members of its subgroup. *B. rostrata* requires clean water, a varied diet, and numerous hiding spots to thrive. It has not been bred in captivity.

Botia rostrata
(Günther, 1868)

Synonyms: none

Common Names: gangetic loach, twin-banded loach, sergeant major botia, botia (Assamese), dohser (Khasi), rani mach (Bengali)

Distribution: India, Bangladesh, Myanmar, China

Occurrences: Irrawaddy River Basin, Myanmar
Salween River Basin, Myanmar
Ganges River Basin, India/Bangladesh
Irrawaddy headwaters, China

Habitat: clear hill streams and creeks that feed larger rivers

Ideal Tank Parameters: pH 6.8 to 7.2; Temp 72° to 79°F (23° to 26°C)

Young *Botia rostrata*.

Botia striata

Botia striata is a very gentle, gregarious fish that should be kept in groups of three or more in a species tank, a community tank, or with other gentle *Botia* species. They are curious and active and do not get too big for most aquarists—about 3 inches (7.8 cm). In nature they experience a range of pH from 6.0 to 8.0. *B. striata* is perhaps the ideal loach for the beginner enthusiast.

Beyond their suitability for a community tank, they are surely one of the most beautiful loaches. Their skin is a pale yellow, growing more silvery toward the belly. Narrow, tightly spaced black or brown vertical bands cross the whole length of the fish, and an even narrower strip of metallic gold separates each band. Interesting variations can occur in the stripes, like "Y" shapes, circles, odd spacing, and so on. These stripes seem to become more compressed and closer together as the fish matures. The head of *B. striata* is particularly attractive, as

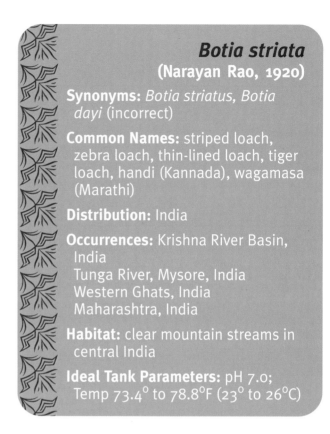

Botia striata
(Narayan Rao, 1920)

Synonyms: *Botia striatus, Botia dayi* (incorrect)

Common Names: striped loach, zebra loach, thin-lined loach, tiger loach, handi (Kannada), wagamasa (Marathi)

Distribution: India

Occurrences: Krishna River Basin, India
Tunga River, Mysore, India
Western Ghats, India
Maharashtra, India

Habitat: clear mountain streams in central India

Ideal Tank Parameters: pH 7.0; Temp 73.4° to 78.8°F (23° to 26°C)

Botia striata.

the vertical banding continues right onto the fish's snout, bisecting each eye. The stripes extend onto the fins. *B. striata* individuals in good health often have redness around the nose, extending into the base of the barbels.

These spectacular and social fish are less retiring than many other *Botia* loaches and are similar to *B. histrionica* in the amount of time they spend out of hiding. Kept in groups in an aquarium with plenty of hiding spots and a soft substrate of fine gravel or sand, they will explore constantly, even swimming in the upper levels of the water column among dither fishes such as danios and White Cloud Mountain minnows.

These loaches are exceptionally easy to feed. They will accept a wide range of foods, including flakes, frozen invertebrates, freeze-dried foods, and fresh vegetables. A mixed diet is essential to their good health.

Genus *Syncrossus*—*Hymenophysa* Complex of Loach Species

Another subgroup of loaches previously classified as *Botia* is known as the "*hymenophysa* complex." Fishes in this group have three pairs of barbels and are generally more slender in appearance. These loaches have been classified as genus *Syncrossus*, an old generic name that has been revived. Members of the genus are very territorial and display their aggressive nature when a tankmate intrudes on their staked-out territory. Members of this genus may sport electric-green bands that run from the snout to the base of the caudal fin, extending down vertically like a tiger's stripes. Additionally, almost all of these loaches, with the exception of *S. helodes*, have small black-spotted markings across the entire body. This dotted pattern fades away in the adult stage of life in all species except *S. berdmorei*.

Syncrossus helodes.

Syncrossus beauforti

Syncrossus beauforti grows to about 4 inches (10 cm) at maturity. This fish appears to grow more rapidly than others in its genus, particularly in early adulthood. Its tendency to nip at other fishes can be a threat to smaller tankmates, so *S. beauforti* may be best suited to the species tank. This fish is also largely nocturnal, so ample shaded spots in the tank are necessary.

This loach bears nine to 12 indistinct gray-green bars along its length. The bars almost all angle toward the rear at their lowest end, with only very slight change towards vertical after the dorsal fin. The body is of almost uniform depth, with little narrowing in the caudal peduncle region. The body color is gray to gray-green, darker at the top and fading to a white belly. The white area reaches higher on the flanks between the head and dorsal fin and is marked with rows of dark spots. The lines of spots are more obvious on the sides and top of the fish's head; variations in these markings offer striking alternatives for the aquarist. The spots, which will remain into adulthood, are elliptical and horizontally oriented but always smaller in size than those on *S. berdmorei*. In adult *S. beauforti*, the vertical banding generally fades and disappears and the fish shows just a brown body base. The dorsal and caudal fins are yellowish to orange in healthy specimens and marked with dots, forming rows of parallel curves. The dorsal fin is distinctly graced with nine soft rays and originates somewhat anterior to the ventral fins. The anal fin is yellowish, with some spots near its base. The eyes, which are quite small in adults, have some red pigment.

During times of flooding along the Mekong River in November and December, waters rise to exceptionally high levels, and this loach can be found swimming in deluged forest areas. The seasonal change in their terrain is significant, as they also enter the Tonle Sap flood plain that affects Cambodia in an annual cycle.

In the aquarium as in the wild, S. *beauforti* prefers small crustaceans such as freshwater shrimp and mollusks such as snails. They are territorial and confrontational fish, not recommended for peaceful tankmates or fishes of a smaller size. Dither fishes also are not recommended. Because these fish are highly sensitive to dissolved organic

Syncrossus beauforti.

Syncrossus beauforti
(Smith, 1931)

Synonyms: *Botia beauforti, Botia lucasbahi*

Common Names: barred loach, Beaufort's loach, chameleon loach, pa keio kai (Laotian), pla moo (Thai), trey damrey (Khmer), trey kanchrouk (Khmer)

Distribution: Indochina

Occurrences: Kompong chang, Cambodia
Stung sam ke River, Cambodia
Prek tasom River, Cambodia
Tonle Sap Lake, Cambodia
Mekong River Basin, Laos
Golok River, Malaysia
Chao Phraya River System, Thailand
Menam Mum River, Thailand
Tadi stream, Thailand
Mekong River Basin, Thailand
Pasa River, Thailand
Mekong River, China
Mekong River, Vietnam

Habitat: inhabits swiftly flowing streams or rivers, of small-to medium-size, with clear water and a gravel or rocky substrate

Ideal Tank Parameters: pH 6 to 6.5; Temp 75° to 82.4°F (24° to 28°C)

compounds (DOCs) and nitrates, *S. beauforti* tank must have clean water and substrate. Frequent gravel cleaning and large water changes will provide a healthy environment.

Syncrossus berdmorei
(Blyth, 1860)

Synonyms: *Botia berdmorei*

Common Names: Blyth's loach

Distribution: India to Thailand

Occurrences: Near Manipur, India
Mandalay Division, Myanmar
Saigang Division, Myanmar
Salween River Basin, Myanmar
Mekong River Basin, Thailand
Myanmar border region, Thailand

Habitat: clear mountain streams as well as medium- to large-size rivers

Ideal Tank Parameters: pH 6.5 to 7.5; Temp 71.6° to 78.8°F (22° to 26°C)

The electric green and iridescent markings of Blyth's loach (*Syncrossus berdmorei*), make it an excellent loach for the species tank.

Syncrossus berdmorei

Another strikingly beautiful yet aggressive fish from the genus *Syncrossus*, *S. berdmorei* grows to a length of nearly 10 inches (25 cm), but generally stays smaller in captivity. This species has only recently become available within the aquarium trade. Distinguishable from the somewhat similar *S. beauforti* by its more dramatic colors and markings, this species remains attractive into adulthood because its striping does not diminish as it matures.

Typical of the *hymenophysa* group, this species has an elongated snout that bears three pairs of barbels. The rostral pair is black in color and connected to the eye by narrow black stripes. There are two prominent black bands behind and over the eyes, which continue along the flanks as a series of short dashes that gradually become elliptical shapes aligned horizontally in parallel rows. The only exception to this is just under the frontal origin point of the dorsal fin, where a series of these ellipses are vertically oriented. The origin of the dorsal fin is slightly behind that of the ventral fins. The rows of dashes and ellipses overlay vertical rows of ten or 11 dark stripes that reflect a metallic greenish hue. The stripes before the dorsal origin are angled slightly toward the rear at

their lower ends. All stripes reach almost to a silver belly. The caudal peduncle area is notably thinner than the rest of the body. The dorsal fin may appear yellowish, with dark transverse bars. The upper edge may show some red coloring, as may the caudal tips. In healthy adults the red intensifies to increase the already attractive appearance.

Because of its beauty at adult size, *S. berdmorei* is a very desirable species if the aggressive side of its nature can be tolerated. Given a large, well-filtered species tank with frequent large water changes, or alternatively mixed with suitably boisterous and resilient companions, a group of this species will make a spectacular display.

Syncrossus berdmorei enjoys flake food, sinking pellets, frozen invertebrates, vegetables, and freeze-dried foods.

Syncrossus helodes

This is a sizable loach from the great rivers of Indochina. Reaching 12 inches (30.5 cm) or more in length, *Syncrossus helodes* spends its long life hunting or scavenging at night. By day it hides and rests amid tangled vegetable matter, tree roots, boulders, and other protected spaces.

Syncrossus helodes is a relatively aggressive fish in the aquarium but can be brought into a community of larger loaches like clowns of a similar mature

Syncrossus helodes
(Sauvage, 1876)

Synonyms: *Botia helodes*

Common Name: banded tiger loach, pa kheo kai (Laotian), trey kanchrouk chhnoht (Khmer)

Distribution: Indochina

Occurrences: Mekong River Basin, Laos/Thailand/Cambodia/Vietnam Tonle Sap Lake, Cambodia Chao Phraya River system, Thailand

Habitat: large tropical river environment, with a substrate of sand, clay, gravel, boulders, and fallen trees

Ideal Tank Parameters: pH: 6 to 6.7; Temp: 75° to 86°F (24° to 30°C)

size. This "tiger" loach bears ten to 12 dark bands on its side and has a shiny silver belly marked by elliptical dark brown to black spots between the throat and anal region. The ellipse are vertical in orientation.

The

Syncrossus helodes.

Syncrossus helodes.

frontal stripes do not extend much below the lateral line, but behind the center of the dorsal they reach progressively farther down to almost reach the belly. The stripes and spots on this loach can shift in the light from dark brown to metallic green, adding to its natural camouflage in nature. Its snout is elongated and the barbels are tender. Coarse gravel can damage the sensory organs of this fish, so a softer substrate is recommended.

Often confused with its cousin *S. hymenophysa*, this species can be distinguished by its longer snout and the dark parallel bands found between the head and dorsal fin that are angled down and toward the back. Behind the dorsal the bands are more vertical. The last band on the caudal peduncle has a prominent black spot at its upper end. Unlike as in *S. hymenophysa*, there is no dorsal spot. The bands lack any blue bordering.

In captivity, *S. helodes* will accept flake food, sinking pellets, frozen invertebrates, vegetables, and freeze-dried foods.

Syncrossus hymenophysa

Reaching an adult size of 8.33 inches (21 cm), this aggressive but beautiful loach should be kept in a species tank or with swift, tough fishes such as larger barb species. Because of its adult size, *Syncrossus hymenophysa* needs plenty of room. A large well-filtered tank with frequent water changes is required.

Syncrossus hymenophysa
(Bleeker, 1852)

Synonyms: *Botia hymenophysa, Botia hymenphysa, Cobitis hymenophysa*

Common Names: tiger loach, green banded loach, pla moo kang lai (Thai), langli (Malay), ca heo (Vietnamese)

Distribution: Borneo and Sumatra, peninsular Malaysia

Occurrences: Kalimantan Timur, Borneo, Indonesia
Indragiri, Sumatra, Indonesia
Belayan River, Borneo, Indonesia
Tahan River, Malaysia
Kuala Teku, Malaysia
Undup River, Sarawak, Borneo, Malaysia

Habitat: lowland streams and lakes, notably on the islands of Sumatra and Borneo

Ideal Tank Parameters: pH 7.0; Temp 77° to 86°F (25° to 30°C)

S. hymenophysa is an elongated, slender loach with a conical pointed head. Its mouth faces downwards, and it has three pairs of barbels. The suborbital spine is forked, and its length is the same as the diameter of the eye. The upper parts of the fish are brown to yellowish-tan and the under parts are pale yellow. The flanks are grayish-yellow or gray-green, marked with 12 to 15 dark transverse bars that sometimes have iridescent blue borders.

The bars between the head and the frontal origin of the dorsal fin are slanted towards the head at the bottom. From the frontal dorsal origin to the end of the caudal peduncle the bars are vertical. These bars reach almost down to the belly, which has no spotting.

The fins are yellowish or greenish, and the dorsal and caudal fins have thin dark bands. The dorsal fin also has a prominent black spot at its upper leading edge.

S. hymenophysa will accept flake foods, sinking pellets, frozen invertebrates, vegetables, and freeze-dried foods and can be quite nippy toward other tank residents during feeding time.

Syncrossus hymenophysa.

Genus *Yasuhikotakia*—Modesta Complex of Loach Species

The "*modesta* complex" is another subgrouping of loaches affected by taxonomic changes in 2004 to the genus *Botia*. These fishes are all classified under the new genus *Yasuhikotakia* and include *Y. caudipunctata, Y. eos, Y. lecontei, Y. modesta, Y. morleti, Y. nigrolineata,* and *Y. sidthimunki.* Most of these loaches are aggressive and territorial. *Y. eos* in particular can be a brute and is capable of killing larger tankmates. Nevertheless, kept in a species tank or with appropriate tankmates of a similar disposition, each of these beautiful and fascinating species can be kept successfully in home aquaria and thrive.

Yasuhikotakia modesta. This genus of loach was named in honor of the Japanese collector and researcher Dr. Yasuhiko Taki.

Yasuhikotakia caudipunctata

Yasuhikotakia caudipunctata is bluish-gray loach that grows to around 3.25 inches (9 cm). The caudal fin is yellow in hue while the dorsal and anal fins have some slight red coloration. The caudal fin is speckled with small black dots. Speckling appears to a lesser degree on the dorsal fin. There is a distinctive dark vertical bar that appears just before the caudal peduncle.

Similar in disposition to its cousins in the "*modesta* complex," *Y. caudipunctata* should be treated as an aggressive fish, perhaps housed with *Y. modesta* or *Y. morleti*. It may also do well among cichlids of a smaller or similar size, but three to five *Y. caudipunctata* alone might be the best alternative. Providing multiple hiding spots is crucial, since these territorial fish need ample refuge.

The speckle-tail loach will accept flake food, sinking tablets, and frozen invertebrates such as bloodworms. They are known to destroy plants, either by grazing the leaves or uprooting them while they excavate the substrate for food.

Yasuhikotakia caudipunctata makes infrequent appearances in the hobby, but these loaches make excellent additions to the semi-aggressive tank.

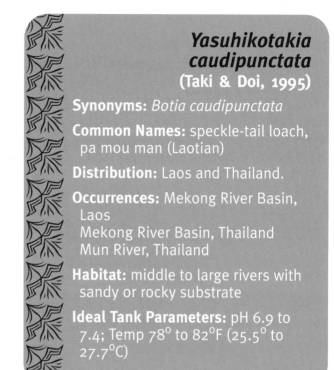

Yasuhikotakia caudipunctata
(Taki & Doi, 1995)

Synonyms: *Botia caudipunctata*

Common Names: speckle-tail loach, pa mou man (Laotian)

Distribution: Laos and Thailand.

Occurrences: Mekong River Basin, Laos
Mekong River Basin, Thailand
Mun River, Thailand

Habitat: middle to large rivers with sandy or rocky substrate

Ideal Tank Parameters: pH 6.9 to 7.4; Temp 78° to 82°F (25.5° to 27.7°C)

Yasuhikotakia eos
(Taki, 1972)

Synonyms: *Botia eos*

Common Names: sun loach, pa mou man (Laotian), trey kanchrouk krawhorm (Khmer), ca heo (Vietnamese)

Distribution: Indochina

Occurrences: Chao Phraya River Basin, Thailand
Maeklong River Basin, Thailand
Nam Ngum River, Laos
Mekong River Basin, Laos/Cambodia/Vietnam
Tonle Sap Lake, Cambodia

Habitat: occurs in rapidly moving water in large and medium size rivers. Inhabits areas with boulders and large gradient gravel substrate

Ideal Tank Parameters: pH 7.0; Temp 75.2° to 82.4°F (24° to 28°C)

Yasuhikotakia eos

Yasuhikotakia eos is an aggressive loach even though it remains rather small at only 4.5 inches (11 cm) maximum length. The body is a light brown, the tail slightly yellow. The dorsal fin is dark red with a black line running along the margins. It looks very similar to the skunk loach (*Y. morleti*) in appearance, but it does not have the black dorsal stripe running along its length. *Y. eos* is also a bit more slender than *Y. morleti* and has 11 soft dorsal rays, whereas *Y. morleti* has 12 or 13.

Y. eos will eat flaked and sinking foods, frozen and live bloodworms, and daphnia, and will probably benefit from some vegetable matter such as cucumber in its diet.

Yasuhikotakia lecontei

Yasuhikotakia lecontei can attain a body length of nearly 6 inches (15 cm) but may remain smaller in the aquarium. Somewhat similar to juvenile *Y. modesta*, its body is more elongated with a flatter

A small but aggressive loach, *Yasuhikotakia eos* should be kept in a species tank or with hardy tankmates.

Yasuhikotakia lecontei
(Fowler, 1937)

Synonyms: *Botia lecontei*

Common Names: silver loach, pa mou man (Laotian), pla moo (Thai), trey kanchrouk loeung (Khmer), ca heo (Vietnamese)

Distribution: Indochina

Occurrences: Mekong River Basin, Laos
Mekong River Basin, Thailand
Chao Phraya River Basin, Thailand
Mun River, Thailand
Mekong River Basin, Cambodia
Mekong River Basin, Vietnam

Habitat: found in fast-moving water in medium to larger rivers with rocky substrate

Ideal Tank Parameters: pH 6.0 to 6.5; Temp 75.2° to 82.4°F (24° to 28°C)

belly profile, particularly in young fish. Its body is a variable brown to yellowish color, but will sometimes appear greenish to delicate blue-gray with a dull silky sheen. There is a dark vertical band at the caudal peduncle; at times this band can be quite visible but at others it is indistinct. Juveniles often have ten to 15 black vertical stripes on the flanks, which fade completely as the fish matures. The fins are yellow to red-orange.

Y. lecontei enjoys frozen brine shrimp, krill, daphnia, and other small crustaceans as well as bloodworms and earthworms. They will eat flake food once acclimated to aquarium life. As with other botiid loaches, variety in their diet is important and will bring out more intense coloring and vigor. They are greedy eaters; overfeeding should be avoided.

Yasuhikotakia modesta

This strikingly colored loach can grow as long as 10 inches, (25 cm) but will rarely exceed 7 inches (18 cm) in the home aquarium. *Yasuhikotakia modesta* needs ample room to swim and forage, so

Yasuhikotakia lecontei.

Yasuhikotakia modesta

(Bleeker, 1865)

Synonyms: *Botia modesta, Botia rubripinnis*

Common Names: red-finned loach, redtail botia, blue botia, ca heo (Vietnamese), keeo gai (Laotian), pa moo mang (Laotian), pla moo (Thai), trey kanchrouk krawhorm (Khmer)

Distribution: Indochina

Occurrences: Mekong River basin, Laos
Chao Phraya River basin, Thailand
Borapet Swamp, Thailand
Mae Khlong River, Thailand
Mekong River basin, Thailand
Bangpakong River, Thailand
Mekong River basin, Cambodia
Tonle Sap Lake, Cambodia
Mekong River basin, Vietnam

Habitat: large rivers with muddy substrate

Ideal Tank Parameters: pH 7.0; Temp 78.8° to 86°F (26° to 30°C)

they are suitable only for tanks of substantial size. Hiding places should be abundant and light levels kept low. Water conditions should be kept as clean as possible through frequent large water changes.

Y. modesta has a compact body with a profoundly arched back. Like *Chromobotia macracanthus*, adult fish are bulky individuals. The caudal fin is forked and all fins are red, orange, or sometimes yellow. The main body color is a bluish-gray. Both the body and fins will become more brightly colored if the fish is in good condition. Some immature specimens can have a greenish appearance to their bodies

In tanks with multiple specimens of *Yasuhikotakia modesta* some sparring can occur, as they develop a pecking order. The least dominant fish in a group may be chased or harassed by the others and relentlessly removed from the better hiding places.

and may be crosshatched by subtle black bars. *Y. modesta* has three pairs of barbels.

In its home waters, *Y. modesta* migrates and can be found in flooded fields in southern Cambodia and the Mekong Delta in Vietnam between May and July. Between November and March it migrates north in the Mekong into tributaries and feeder streams where they spawn.

Juvenile *Y. modesta* are very active fish, moving about their surroundings in schools and interacting with their tankmates. However, as they reach adulthood they become more reclusive and the majority of their time is spent hiding in caves or other areas. At night *Y. modesta* emerges and actively swims around the aquarium; individuals then chase one another and root in the gravel for bits of leftover food. At these times they can be quite loud, emitting clicks of startling volume. Because of its robust activity, tankmates for this species must be chosen wisely.

Talented diggers, these fish should be kept in aquaria with a soft substrate of fine gravel or sand. Sometimes rooted plants are dug up, so it may be better to keep *Y. modesta* with plants that can be secured to rocks or wood, such as Java fern or *Anubias* species.

This photograph depicts the horrors that dyed fish are subjected to. These poor specimens of *Yasuhikotakia modesta* have been cruelly and pointlessly dyed garish colors prior to their arrival in North America. Fish that are dyed artificially should be avoided, and retailers who attempt to sell them should be avoided as well.

Yasuhikotakia modesta.

Females are generally rounder than males and their bodies may be lighter in color. *Y. modesta* has not been successfully bred in captivity. Artificial coloring of these fish sometimes occurs in the aquarium trade, attempting to enhance the species' already attractive coloration. Two methods seem to be used. The first is feeding of an artificial color-enhancing food designed to bring out the intensity of blue pigment in the fish's body and red pigment in the fins. The second—and more abhorrent—method is by somehow dyeing the fish or injecting dyes into the fish's skin. The results of both of these practices are temporary. The fish returns to its natural hues once the color- enhancing food is no longer being fed, and dye is eventually metabolized, leading to patchy coloration at best or, at worst, the introduction of infection via the injection site. These practices severely compromise the health of the fish. Purchase of these artificially enhanced animals is completely discouraged because of these factors.

Care should be taken that food is provided to each individual fish when kept in a group, since less dominant fish may be denied their fair share. Feeding small portions at several discrete locations within the tank allows these less dominant fish to avoid having to compete for food and may cut down on aggressive behavior. These loaches enjoy brine shrimp, krill, bloodworms, earthworms, *Daphnia,* and other small invertebrates and even live adult insects. They may become accustomed to flake food, but variety in their diet is important and will bring out more intense coloring. *Y. modesta* individuals are extremely avid eaters, so overfeeding should be avoided.

Yasuhikotakia morleti

A smaller loach, reaching only about 4 inches (10 cm), *Yasuhikotakia morleti* is very territorial and defensive. This fish is noted for active production of clicking sounds during its social interactions or when feeding. The body is grayish-pink to yellowish-green in color, with a paler belly area. It is more laterally compressed than most other botiid species, with a pronounced arched back. The dorsal fin is positioned directly parallel to the ventral fins. An intense black line runs down the spine from nose to tail and then forms a thicker vertical line down the caudal peduncle. This is the single most distinguishing feature of the species. The flanks may show four indistinct short thin vertical bars. All the fins are translucent gray, and there is some yellow coloring in the tail, which occasionally has dark spots. In mature individuals from some populations the pectoral, ventral, and anal fins have an orange color.

Although juveniles tend to be more active during the day, this loach is largely nocturnal and should

Yasuhikotakia morleti
(Tirant, 1885)

Synonyms: *Botia morleti, Botia horae*

Common Names: skunk loach, Hora's loach, cream loach, trey kanchrouk (Khmer)

Distribution: Indochina

Occurrences: Mekong River Basin, Laos
Mekong River Basin, Thailand
Chao Phraya River Basin, Thailand
Tapi River, Thailand
Mekong River Basin, Cambodia
Tonle Sap Lake, Cambodia
Mekong River Basin, Vietnam

Habitat: inhabits medium to large rivers, but in areas with slow-moving to still waters, with sandy substrate

Ideal Tank Parameters: pH 7.0; Temp 78.8° to 83°F (26° to 30°C)

Yasuhikotakia morleti.

be provided with numerous hiding spots such as rocky caves, tree roots, and driftwood. They are very good at digging and excavate the substrate in search of food, so a soft substrate is necessary. As a result of their frequent digging, rooted plants are probably not suited for the skunk loach tank. However, some *Anubias* species and Java fern may be affixed to rocks or wood décor in the tank, where they will remain unharmed.

Because *Y. morleti* hails from still pools in larger rivers, increased circulation is not necessary in the aquarium. When its water is kept clean through frequent large water changes, this hardy loach can actually withstand a wide variety of water chemistries. The species has been recorded in nature inhabiting a pH range from 6.0 to 8.0, though neutral pH in slightly soft water is ideal.

Y. morleti is regularly available in the aquarium trade, but some thought should be given to its purchase. Because of the extremely aggressive and territorial nature of this species, care should be given when choosing potential tankmates. Faster fishes such as barbs, tetras, and some species of rainbowfish are ideal. One should avoid any long-finned fish such as angelfish or bettas. They can be kept in small groups with other skunk loaches, but fighting will take place between them unless they are offered a tank with a large floor area. Additional hiding spots will reduce their aggressive behavior. In a large tank they may be combined in small numbers with other aggressive loach species, such as *Y. modesta* or *Y. lecontei*.

This loach should be fed lightly. Individuals have been known to gorge to the point where they cause themselves harm, even to die from overeating. Flake food will be accepted, but they thrive on a varied diet of frozen or freeze-dried invertebrates, or live snails.

Yasuhikotakia nigrolineata

Yasuhikotakia nigrolineata is found in the creeks and streams that feed the Mekong and Chao Phraya rivers between Yunnan, China and northern Thailand. Their natural environment is the fast-flowing subtropical stream. They have been found in water ranging from 59° to 77°F (15° to 25°C). For aquarium purposes, one should aim for the middle of this temperature range, with neutral water that is kept sparkling clean with a rapid flow rate. A river tank setup may be an ideal home for *Y. nigrolineata*. At the very least, one or more powerheads should be added to their environment to provide substantially higher water flow.

The black-lined loach is distinguished by the black horizontal stripe that runs the length of the fish from the tip of the snout to the caudal base. In

Yasuhikotakia nigrolineata
(Kottelat & Chu, 1987)

Synonyms: *Botia nigrolineata*

Common Names: black-lined loach

Distribution: Southern China to Thailand

Occurrences: Mekong River Basin, China
Mekong River Basin, Laos
Mekong River Basin, Thailand
Chao Phraya River Basin, Thailand

Habitat: found in small creeks and streams with sandy substrate and moderate to fast-moving clear water

Ideal Tank Parameters: pH 7.0 to 7.5; Temp 65° to 70°F (18° to 21°C)

The parallel black lines on *Yasuhikotakia nigrolineata* remain mostly separate, unlike *Y. sidthimunki*.

juveniles this is a prominent feature. While some adolescent wild-caught specimens may display signs of vertical banding, these generally fade and leave the single black line on each flank. The head of *Y. nigrolineata* is triangular in shape and pointed, similar to that of *Y. sidthimunki*. They have four pairs of barbels. The dorsal fin, almost perfectly triangular in shape, is quite tall when erect. The oval pelvic fins are wide, enabling the fish to "hover" in the water. When in excellent health, *Y. nigrolineata* will take on a yellowish-gold metallic hue to the normally cream-colored body.

This is a smaller loach that grows to about 4 inches (10 cm). It should be kept in groups of three or more and will likely do better in larger numbers in the aquarium. A social loach, *Y. nigrolineata* will interact with others of its species, but it largely ignores other tankmates. Much time is spent schooling, though individuals will seek solitary refuge occasionally if ample hiding spots are provided. They will also burrow, so some parts of the tank should have a sand or fine gravel substrate. Plants are also welcome in the tank. As juveniles they will hide among the leaves and stems, and adults will graze the leaves for algae, small invertebrates, and other food sources.

Brine shrimp, bloodworms, live earthworms, and other "meaty" items may be the only foods

Yasuhikotakia sidthimunki.

accepted by *Y. nigrolineata.* They should not be kept with long-finned fishes such as bettas, gouramis, and angelfish because in a group the black-lined loaches may be tempted to pursue such fishes like a pack of wolves. They get along well with other peaceful loaches such as *Botia dario, B. histrionica,* and *Chromobotia macracanthus.*

Yasuhikotakia sidthimunki

   Yasuhikotakia sidthimunki is the smallest of the botiid loaches and rarely exceeds 2.25 inches (5.5 cm) in length. A small, attractive fish that often schools high into the water column, it is very desirable. Dwarf loaches are now listed on the IUCN Red List as critically endangered, and they are a protected species in Thailand. These fish do not seem to breed in the tank setting, but numerous

Yasuhikotakia sidthimunki
(Klausewitz, 1959)

Synonyms: *Botia sidthimunki*

Common Names: dwarf loach, chained loach, ladderback loach

Distribution: Indochina

Occurrences: Chao Phraya River Basin, Thailand
Kwai river Basin, Thailand
Mae Klong River Basin, Thailand

Habitat: medium to larger rivers, flooded fields, and small muddy lakes, standing water

Ideal Tank Parameters: pH 6.6 to 7.2; Temp 78.8° to 82.4°F (26° to 28°C)

Two specimens of the dwarf loach (*Yasuhikotakia sidthimunki*). The one on the right is "grayed out."

efforts are underway to unlock the secrets of their reproductive and hormonal cycles. Successful breeding programs would not only increase their availability to the aquarium trade but also may allow for reintroduction into their natural habitat.

As with all other botiid species, a large tank with very clean water suits *Y. sidthimunki*. Frequent large water changes and a healthy biological filter in the tank will prevent the buildup of ammonia or nitrite. A medium to high level of water flow will simulate their habitat and increase the amount of time they spend schooling together. As with other loaches, many hiding spots should be provided. Plants, driftwood, rock caves, and other variations should be available in the tank.

Dwarf loaches will accept a wide range of foods, but bloodworms are a clear favorite.

The small size of individual *Y. sidthimunki* may allow them to enter the filter apparatus more

> *The International Union for Conservation of Nature and Natural Resources considers* Yasuhikotakia sidthimunki *to be facing "an extremely high risk of extinction in the wild." For more information on the species listed on the IUCN Red List and the criteria for their inclusion visit www.redlist.org.*

easily, so care should be taken that intake tubes are covered in fine nylon mesh, sponges, or similar material. The tank hood should be secured tightly to prevent the fish from leaping out.

Y. sidthimunki is often confused with a similar but separate species, *Y. nigrolineata*. Though once considered a subspecies of *Y. sidthimunki*, *Y. nigrolineata* was reclassified as a distinct species in 1987. *Y. sidthimunki* is distinct in that on each flank there are two black horizontal stripes that start at the head and end at the caudal peduncle. Several shorter black bands extend vertically down from the back of the fish to the black horizontal stripe, thereby creating the appearance of a chain-like pattern, hence one of the species's common names. The basic body coloration of *Y. sidthimunki* may vary, though most individuals have a shiny silver appearance.

Genus *Sinibotia*—Chinese Complex of Loach Species

This complex of loaches is found primarily in Chinese rivers and streams, in swiftly moving water. Found in cooler waters, in areas that experience at least a short winter, these are some of the subtropical loaches. All species in this category are now considered members of the genus *Sinibotia*; they were previously known as species of the genus *Botia*.

Sinibotia longiventralis

This species has an elongated botiid shape and may reach a length in excess of 4.25 inches (10.6 cm). Unlike as with many other botiid loaches, the body is extremely flexible and eel-like. This enables *Sinibotia longiventralis* to swim in a fashion similar to that of kuhli loaches, pushing themselves through impossibly tight gaps, making sharp turns around rocks, pebbles, or other obstacles. The body of *S. longiventralis* is generally deep maroon in color, sporting seven to 12 bright golden bands that are aligned vertically across the fish. In juveniles the pigmentation appears light red. As the loach ages, the pigmentation darkens to a deeper red. *S. longiventralis* also has a red tint to the barbels and snout.

Found primarily in Yunnan in the upper reaches of the Mekong River system, but extending as far south as the Lao-Thai border, this loach may be an excellent addition to the hillstream tank. While not true hillstreams (i.e., Balitoridae), they will benefit from cooler temperatures and faster water flow. They are peaceful and seem to get along with most other non-aggressive fish species. Sometimes aloof, they may not interact at all, let alone school, with other members of their own kind.

Like the *Acanthocobitis* species of loaches, they have a very keen sense of smell. They will detect

Sinibotia longiventralis
(Yang & Chen, 1992)

Synonyms: *Botia longiventralis*

Common Names: Chinese zebra loach

Distribution: Southern China and the upper Mekong

Occurrences: Mekong River Basin, Yunnan, China
Mekong River Basin, Laos
Mekong River Basin, Thailand

Habitat: streams and rivers with rocky substrate, high water flow, and cooler temperatures

Ideal Tank Parameters: pH 6.7 to 7.4; Temp 69° to 75°F (20.5° to 23.8°C)

food soon after it is placed into the tank—darting up to the surface to snatch a morsel and then retreating to a sheltered area to devour their catch. *S. longiventralis* will accept live or frozen invertebrates, algae wafers, and even flake food.

Sinibotia robusta

Sinibotia robusta is distinguished from similar-looking members of the genus by six or seven prominent black bars that stretch vertically from the dorsal area to the belly. The four middle bands are distinctive in the way they split at about the lateral line into two points that continue down to the silvery belly. The body of the *S. robusta* is sandy in color along the back, fading down into metallic yellowish-silver. Under certain lighting

Sinibotia pulchra has a flexible body and moves like an eel between rocks and plants in the aquarium.

Sinibotia robusta.

Sinibotia robusta
(Wu, 1939)

Synonyms: *Botia robusta, Botia hexafurca*

Common Names: Chinese golden zebra loach

Distribution: Southern China and the extreme north of Vietnam

Occurrences: Song Hong River Basin, China
Song Hong River Basin, Vietnam

Habitat: fast water movement, rocky substrate, cool temperatures; has been recorded in brackish waters

Ideal Tank Parameters: pH 7.0 to 7.8; Temp 64.4° to 75.2°F (18° to 24°C)

conditions the fish can appear to be a light gold color. The head is significantly elongated like that of most other *Sinibotia*, but the body is much more compact and proportionately shorter than in all other *Sinibotia* species. *S. robusta* grows to 3.5 inches (8.8 cm). The fins are basically colorless, with some delicate black banding on each ray. The dorsal fin has a single fairly wide black band marked on each fin ray. This is wider at the front of the fin, narrowing as it arcs downward to where it meets the back.

S. robusta is a territorial loach that will exhibit aggression if it is crowded. A larger aquarium with perhaps eight to ten hiding spots per fish is most suitable. Plants are also highly recommended, since these fish will swim around the clock in search of snails and other invertebrates that collect around vegetation. They are extremely inquisitive, accept

This image of two specimens of *Sinibotia robusta* clearly shows how the markings develop as the fish matures.

most foods, and will sit on the bottom of the tank resting on their fins, turning their head from side to side, always on the lookout for a tasty morsel.

Genus *Leptobotia*

Very few species of *Leptobotia* appear on the aquarium market. One exception is the Chinese golden tiger loach, *Leptobotia guilinensis*.

The rarely seen *Leptobotia mantschurica*.

Leptobotia guilinensis

Like *Sinibotia longiventralis,* this species has an elongated, flexible, eel-like body. Individuals are extremely agile when searching the aquarium for food. Lightning-fast swimmers possessing an ultra-sensitive sense of smell, they will rush around the aquarium as soon as food is introduced. Flake, pellet food, thawed frozen foods, and live foods are all eagerly accepted. Between feeding times the fish

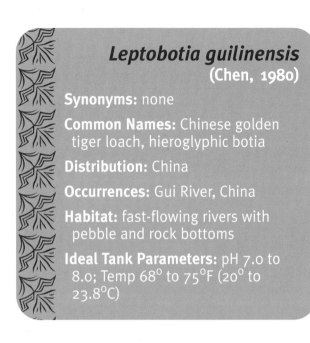

Leptobotia guilinensis
(Chen, 1980)

Synonyms: none

Common Names: Chinese golden tiger loach, hieroglyphic botia

Distribution: China

Occurrences: Gui River, China

Habitat: fast-flowing rivers with pebble and rock bottoms

Ideal Tank Parameters: pH 7.0 to 8.0; Temp 68° to 75°F (20° to 23.8°C)

will rest up in tight-fitting spots or fiddle around the tank, searching everywhere for any tasty hidden items. They are quite active diggers and will bury their snouts into the substrate, right up to the eyes, if they detect a morsel below the surface.

This is an attractively marked and colored loach. The base color is a rich yellow, fading to silver on the belly. The body is marked by 12 to 15 dark brown bars that are extremely variable in width and spacing. The bars are sometimes bisected by lighter stripes or form a "Y" shape. In most cases the dark stripes are wider than the intervals between them. In older fish, the gill plates and cheeks become progressively more marked with dark spots and lines, forming a network across the head. When fully grown they reach an adult length

Leptobotia cf. *guilinensis*.

Parabotia maculosa.

of about 4 inches (10 cm). There is extreme variability in markings between individual fish.

A peaceful species, *L. guilinensis* will cohabitate safely with its own species and others. The streams in their natural habitat are fast flowing and generally cooler, making this species ideally suited for inclusion in a river tank type environment. They will live happily with smaller hillstream species, but care must be taken that the hungry *Leptobotia* do not get all the food.

Genus *Parabotia*

Specimens of this genus may appear from time to time, mixed in with other ornamental fishes, particularly in shipments arriving from southern China or Vietnam. Presently, though, they are not popular in the aquarium trade and little is known about their care. The species of *Parabotia* have elongated narrow bodies, often with uniform vertical banding from snout to tail. Some of the Chinese species experience winter in their range, so they may do well in an unheated river tank.

Loaches

Chapter 8

The Family Cobitidae

Loaches that have suborbital spines but lack the fairly consistent body shape of members of the family Botiidae are found in the family Cobitidae. This group of fishes is diverse indeed, ranging from the tiny kuhli loaches (*Pangio* spp.) to the sizable horseface loach (*Acantopsis choirorhynchus*) and weather loach (*Misgurnus anguillicaudatus*).

Genus *Pangio*—Kuhli Loaches

Loaches are one of the most variable families of fish when it comes to size and appearance, and the kuhli loaches are among the most interesting examples. At first glance these animals resemble earthworms more than fishes, but make no mistake: they are all loach. Native primarily to Indonesia and Southeast Asia, kuhlis are small bottom-dwelling fishes, usually with three pairs of barbels around the mouth. They have small black or brown eyes (depending on the species) that are covered with a protective membrane, and they have sharp suborbital spines used for defense.

Kuhlis range in color from a chocolate brown and metallic gold to the most commonly seen variety of pale yellowish-pink or orange with black vertical

On *Pangio kuhlii* and *P. semicincta*

Though they look similar, specimens collected from the streams and rivers of Sumatra, Malaysia, and Borneo previously considered *P. kuhlii* are now classified as *P. semicincta*. To determine with certainty whether a loach is *P. kuhlii* or *P. semicincta*, one must know the exact locality where the fish was collected. To complicate things further, the possibility exists for captive crossbreedings that give rise to hybrids that would not normally occur in the wild.

stripes. The Indonesian name for these little fishes is "tali-tali" which roughly translated into English means "rope" or "string."

There are a number of very similar-looking striped species in the genus *Pangio,* but only one carries the moniker "kuhli" in its Latin name. *P.*

Pangio agma grows to about 2.5 inches (6.3 cm).

kuhlii is a 3.5- to 4-inch (9- to 10-cm) fish with nine to 13 black bars on its flanks that almost circle the body but stop at the belly. This species is found only on the Indonesian island of Java.

The patterns of the striped kuhlis can vary greatly between individuals and among members of the same species. The differences can be very subtle, so exact identification can be a challenge. For most aquarists and certainly for the kuhlis themselves, these scientific distinctions have little meaning. Kuhlis of all colors and patterns will happily live together and peacefully interact in the home aquarium. For the sake of simplicity, this chapter will refer to all those fishes commonly sold under the name "kuhli loach" as kuhlis.

Water Conditions

These mild-mannered fishes make a great addition to almost any freshwater aquarium, but they are not a species for those new to the aquarium hobby. Kuhlis require a well-established tank with excellent water quality; even trace amounts of ammonia or nitrite can be lethal. Good filtration with moderate water movement is essential. Like most other loaches, kuhlis have a low tolerance for elevated levels of nitrate and dissolved organic compounds. They accept a wide range of water chemistry but seem to prefer soft, well-oxygenated, slightly acidic water with a pH of 6.2 to 6.8. Quality and stability are the keys to success when keeping kuhli loaches. A buffer is recommended to

The Kahang, Johor, Malaysia. Leaf litter and shore vegetation are found in the slower water flow. Six species of *Pangio* are found here.

keep the pH and hardness from fluctuating. Most kuhlis do best if housed at temperatures between 78° and 82°F (25.5° and 28°C). One exception is *P. shelfordi*, which needs cooler temperatures between 72° and 77°F (22° and 25°C).

Treatment

Care should be taken when introducing newly purchased kuhli loaches. As of this writing the majority found in the aquarium trade are wild-caught. Use of a cycled quarantine tank is a must, and the initial acclimation procedure should not be rushed. It is highly recommended that all new arrivals be treated for internal and external parasites during quarantine even if they do not show any outward signs of illness.

Like other loaches, kuhlis have scales, but those scales are extremely small. Having such tiny scales means that substances in the water are more readily absorbed by kuhlis than other fishes. Of all the loaches, kuhlis are among the most sensitive to medications; negative reactions can be unpredictable, particularly with anti-parasite remedies. With the exception of antibiotics, it is recommended that half doses be administered until it is clear whether a given kuhli can tolerate the treatment. If the label recommends halving the dose for "sensitive" or "scaleless" fish, the directions should be followed accordingly. If a copper preparation is used to treat for external parasites, use a chelated form. Non-chelated forms of copper have proven fatal to kuhlis.

Some aquarists have also reported serious adverse effects in loaches, particularly kuhlis, when using treatments containing tea tree oil (*Melaleuca alternifolia*) or bay rum (*Pimenta racemosa*) despite

Pangio myersi.

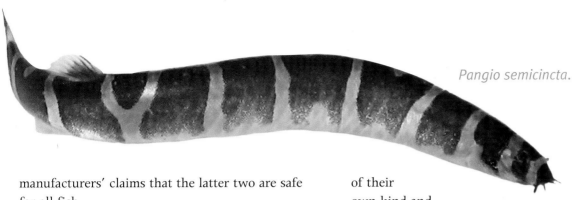

Pangio semicincta.

manufacturers' claims that the latter two are safe for all fish.

Those kuhli loaches that survive quarantine usually go on to live long, healthy lives. Once past the initial acclimation period, kuhlis have proven to be hardy fish when kept in the correct conditions. The average lifespan is uncertain, but one hobbyist reported that a kuhli he had long thought perished was discovered beneath his under gravel filter as he was tearing down the tank. He had purchased the fish 15 years earlier!

A Good Neighbor and Friend

Kuhli loaches are ideal additions to the peaceful community tank. They should not be housed with aggressive or carnivorous fishes that are big enough to eat them and may view them as food. Fishes like puffers and the larger cichlids such as oscars are inappropriate tankmates. Good candidates for sharing a home with kuhlis include other non-aggressive loaches like the clown (*Chromobotia macracanthus*), yoyo (*Botia almorhae*), Bengal (*B. dario*), Burmese (*B. kubotai*), twin-banded (*B. rostrata*), zebra (*B. striata*), gold zebra (*B. histronica*), zipper (*Acanthocobitis botia*), dojo (*Misgurnus anguillicaudatus*), and horseface (*Acantopsis choirorhynchus*) loaches. Other compatible species include corydoras, discus, barbs, danios, rasboras, rainbowfish, livebearers, White Clouds, tetras, and the smaller suckermouth catfishes like the *Otocinclus* and *Peckoltia* species.

Kuhlis are social animals that enjoy the company of their own kind and should be kept in groups of three or more. When kept in small groups in a tank with plenty of plants and hiding places, kuhlis will feel secure and the aquarist will be rewarded by regularly seeing them out in the open swimming and searching for food. They will drape themselves within vegetation by using the leaves like a hammock, or pile up together in small caves or at the base of plants, lying on their sides to nap.

Behavior

Like other loaches, kuhlis often exhibit quirky behaviors. They like to sleep in awkward positions and in unusual spots. Newly introduced kuhlis

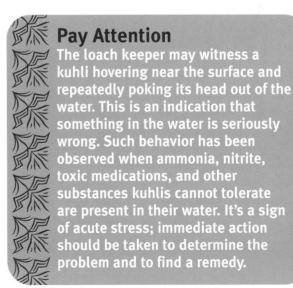

Pay Attention
The loach keeper may witness a kuhli hovering near the surface and repeatedly poking its head out of the water. This is an indication that something in the water is seriously wrong. Such behavior has been observed when ammonia, nitrite, toxic medications, and other substances kuhlis cannot tolerate are present in their water. It's a sign of acute stress; immediate action should be taken to determine the problem and to find a remedy.

Loaches

often will swim up and down the sides of their tank almost as if they are pacing. This behavior is also frequently seen after a water change and is considered to be a reaction to even slight changes in water chemistry or temperature.

It can be a challenge for the aquarist new to kuhlis to determine what behavior is normal and what is not. The only way to be certain is to watch them closely and become familiar with their habits and behaviors. Eventually their behavior becomes more understandable.

Kuhlis are curious fish and have been known to wriggle beneath undergravel filter plates, inside of decorations, and into filter intakes, usually with fatal consequences. Any hole or crack that may present a danger or a means of escape should be covered. Even the smallest opening should be scrutinized. Pre-filter sponges can be used to cover filter openings. Plastic mesh can be cut to any desired shape and attached to decorations over hazardous openings by using aquarium-safe silicone. Once the silicone is fully cured, this

method will allow water to flow through while at the same time keeping the kuhlis safe from harm. Kuhlis have also been known to jump, so the tank should be securely covered with a canopy or glass top.

Kuhlis are one of the burrowing loaches and will enjoy a sand substrate, though it is not essential to their survival. If using gravel, it should be small to medium in size and of a smooth, round grain so as not to cause abrasions or injure the kuhlis' tender barbels as they dig and forage for food. In the wild, kuhlis are largely nocturnal animals, but if they are kept in a tank with subdued lighting and ample hiding spots, they will be seen throughout the day and will be most active at feeding times.

Habitat

The kuhli loach's natural habitat consists of slow flowing rivers and streams. The substrate is usually a sandy bottom with a thick layer of peat, leaf litter and dense plants where they like to congregate. Aquarium grade peat or dried oak leaves can be

Pangio semicineta.

added to the aquarium to better replicate their natural habitat. While captive kuhli loaches will no doubt enjoy mucking about in peat or leaves on the bottom of their tank, the aquarist may not be quite so fond of this. Oak leaves decompose and break apart, making a mess of the water column and clogging filters. Peat tends to tint the water a brown tea color and can make maintenance difficult. More importantly, peat will alter water chemistry by making it more acidic. In a closed system like a fish tank this can happen very quickly, and such a rapid change in water chemistry can be deadly to the fish. How much changing of the water's composition a given amount of peat will cause is difficult to predict. Its use is something to be considered only by very experienced aquarists.

One solution employed by loach keepers who want to use peat is to mix pure milled sphagnum peat into the sandy substrate during the original setup of the tank. This allows some of the peat to eventually find its way to the surface of the sand where the kuhlis can then have access to it.

Breeding

Sexing kuhlis is difficult. In general, females are thought to be slightly fatter, especially through the belly, while males are thinner and may have larger pectoral fins. Breeding kuhli loaches in captivity is rare and usually accidental. When it does occur, it is preceded by the female's becoming visibly gravid and swollen with eggs. The male begins courting the female by coiling his body around hers, and the two eventually engage in parallel swimming. At that point the female deposits her bright green eggs in floating vegetation.

The incubation period for the eggs at 80°F (26.6°C) is approximately 24 hours. To decrease the chances of predation and improve the odds of

rearing the fry to adulthood, the eggs should be carefully moved to a breeding net or separate tank with identical water parameters. The use of an eyedropper can make this task a bit easier.

Newly hatched fry are tiny, with external fruticose gills that disappear in ten to 14 days. Fry can initially be fed brine shrimp nauplii and, when they are a little larger, chopped bloodworms. At one month of age they should be large enough to be introduced back into the aquarium, but measures should be taken to prevent any juveniles from being swallowed by filter intakes. Be cautious when siphoning the substrate during regular maintenance. It is advisable to run the siphon into a large bucket rather than directly to the drain. That way, any juveniles accidentally captured by the siphon can be retrieved from the bucket and returned to the tank.

Food

Kuhli loaches are omnivorous and will accept a wide variety of foods including flake and frozen foods. Individual tastes can vary, but favorites include bloodworms, brine shrimp, and sinking algae wafers. Though some are known to enjoy fresh cucumber, kuhlis will not eat aquarium vegetation. This makes them excellent candidates for the planted tank. Also, their scavenging nature actually helps to reduce pollutants in the water, as they seem to locate and devour every crumb of food that enters the tank or is left uneaten by other fish.

Praise for Kuhlis

Kuhli loaches are a wonderful eye-catching addition to the non-aggressive community tank. If kept in the proper conditions, their comical antics will provide the aquarist with years of pleasure and enjoyment.

Species Descriptions

There are approximately two dozen known kuhli loach species, though only a handful of them are regularly found in the aquarium trade. Those described here are the ones most likely to be seen in the tanks at the local fish store.

Pangio anguillaris

Less robust than the other kuhli species, *Pangio anguillaris* is a thin ribbon-like fish that moves along the bottom of the aquarium much like a snake. There is no nasal barbel. The body coloration is a sandy-yellow or finely spotted golden-brown. A faint sky blue stripe runs along the side from the gill opening to the caudal fin. The anal fin sometimes takes on a reddish hue. Even though *P. anguillaris* is not an albino variation of any *Pangio*, it is sometimes incorrectly sold under the name "albino kuhli loach." *P. anguillaris* is more diurnal than other members of its genus and is frequently observed out in the open. This fish is

Pangio anguillaris.

Pangio anguillaris
(Vaillant, 1902)

Synonyms: *Acanthophthalmus anguillaris, Acanthophthalmus vermicularis, Cobitophis anguillaris, Cobitophis perakensis*

Common Names: albino kuhli loach, eel loach, golden kuhli loach, pla ard (Thai)

Distribution: Indochina, Malay Peninsula, Sumatra and Borneo

Occurrences: Mekong River Basin, Cambodia
Dangtong River, Cambodia
Mekong River Basin, Thailand
Mae Nam Nan River, Thailand
Ping River, Thailand
Kwai Noi River, Thailand
Meklong River Basin, Thailand
Chao Praya River Basin, Thailand
Perak River Basin, Malaysia

Habitat: found on or near the bottom of medium- to large-size rivers in stretches with slow current and a sand or silt substrate with leaf litter

Ideal Tank Parameters: pH: 5.0 to 6.0; Temp 76° to 79°F (24° to 26°C)

one of the more skittish kuhlis so it needs lots of hiding spots and tends to bury itself in the sand more than other types. A very social fish, *P. anguillaris* individuals seem to groom each other. While one fish remains motionless the other nibbles away at the flank, apparently eating or cleaning away dirt that may have accumulated. This behavior has not been observed in other *Pangio* species. Surprisingly, sparring does occur among individuals of this species; it is only rarely that injury results from such scuffles.

P. anguillaris spends much of its time buried in the sand or slowly foraging across its surface. This fish breeds in very shallow water with a lot of vegetation, most commonly in flooded forests or grasslands along the water's edge.

This species prefers more meaty foods such as frozen bloodworms or chopped earthworms. It does not seem to readily accept flake foods and may even starve to death if flake is the only type of food offered.

Keep in groups of three or more. This loach reaches a maximum size of 4.75 inches (12 cm).

Pangio cuneovirgata

Color pattern consists of approximately 14 short black saddles restricted to the dorsal half of body, with a dark stripe running down the back connecting them. There is a vertical black bar at the base of the caudal fin. The three bars on head and the ones posterior to the anal fin are somewhat longer than the others. The belly is white and takes on a pearly sheen in gravid females. The dorsal half

Pangio cuneovirgata.

of the body has yellowish background coloration. The female's pectoral fins are smaller, and males have a thickened second ray on the pectoral fin. The tail is transparent and has no markings. The anal fin begins behind the distal end of the dorsal fin. The anterior nostril is pierced at the anterior base of a long nasal barbel.

Pangio cuneovirgata can be distinguished from the other banded kuhlis by this nasal barbel and its truncated caudal fin. *P. cuneovirgata* is omnivorous and requires a diet with a wide variety of foods including flake and frozen foods. Favorite foods include bloodworms, brine shrimp, and sinking algae wafers. They are social loaches and should be kept in groups of three or more. *P. cuneovirgata* reaches a maximum size of 3.125 inches (8 cm).

Pangio cuneovirgata
(Raut, 1957)

Synonyms: *Acanthophthalmus cuneovirgata, Pangio robiginosa*

Common Names: none

Distribution: Malay Peninsula, Sumatra, and West Java

Occurrences: Sai Buri River, Thailand
Sembrong River, Malaysia

Habitat: found among submerged vegetation and leaf litter along the banks of streams with moderate current and clear water. Coexists with *P. semicincta*

Ideal Tank Parameters: pH: 6.2 to 7.0; Temp 78° to 82°F (25.5° to 28°C)

Pangio kuhlii

A yellow-orange to delicate salmon pink fish with nine to 13 dark brown to deep black bars (the first three are on the head) usually irregular and wider dorsally. The bars may be split up the middle by a pale streak and reach nearly to the underside. The intervals are narrower than the bars and the belly is paler in color. There is a large quadrangular blotch occupying the proximal half of caudal fin. The median lobe of the lower lip is not produced into a barbel.

P. kuhlii requires a diet that includes flake and frozen foods. Favorites include bloodworms, brine shrimp, and sinking algae wafers. They should be kept in groups of three or more. *P. kuhlii* reaches maturity at 2.75 inches (7 cm) but can grow up to 4.75 inches (12 cm) in total length.

Pangio kuhlii
(Valenciennes, 1846)

Synonyms: *Acanthophthalmus kuhlii, Cobitis kuhlii*

Common Names: coolie loach, kuhli loach, leopard eel, prickly-eye, thorn-eye, tali-tali (Javanese)

Distribution: Island of Java

Occurrences: Batavia, Java, Indonesia

Habitat: found among submerged vegetation and decaying plant matter in streams with moderate current and clear water

Ideal Tank Parameters: pH: 6.2 to 6.8; Temp 78° to 82°F (25.5° to 28°C)

Pangio kuhlii.

Pangio malayana

Pangio malayana has color patterns consisting of approximately ten to 16 short black saddles restricted to the dorsal half of body. There is an incomplete black bar at the base of the caudal fin. This kuhli is further distinguished from other similar-looking species by the second bar on its head, which, unlike as in *P. kuhlii, P. semicincta,* and *P. cuneovirgata,* does not meet ventrally behind the lower lip. The dorsal half of the body has yellow-orange background coloration; the belly is paler in color. The female's pectoral fins are smaller, and the male's pectoral fins have a thickened second ray. The tail is transparent and without markings. The anal fin begins behind the distal end of the dorsal fin.

This kuhli is omnivorous and requires a diet with a wide variety of foods including flake and frozen

Pangio malayana
(Tweedie, 1956)

Synonyms: *Acanthophthalmus kuhlii malayanus*

Common Names: none

Distribution: Malaysia, Borneo, Sumatra and southernmost peninsular Thailand

Occurrences: Tahan River, Pahang, Malaysia

Habitat: lives on the bottom of sandy forest streams among heavy vegetation. Prefers warmer waters

Ideal Tank Parameters: pH: 6.2 to 6.8; Temp 78° to 85° F (25.5° to 29°C)

Pangio malayana.

Pangio myersi
(Harry, 1949)

Synonyms: *Acanthophthalmus myersi*

Common Names: giant kuhli, Myer's loach, Myer's slimy loach, slimy loach

Distribution: Indochina

Occurrences: Menam Chantaburi River, Thailand
Mekong River Basin, Thailand/Laos/Cambodia

Habitat: lives on the bottom of sandy or muddy creeks and streams among leaf litter or heavy vegetation

Ideal Tank Parameters: pH: 6.2 to 7.0; Temp 79° to 83° F (26° to 28°C)

foods. Favorite items include bloodworms, brine shrimp, and sinking algae wafers. Keep *P. malayana* in groups of three or more. This species reaches a maximum size of 3.125 inches (8 cm).

Pangio myersi

This *Pangio* is heavier bodied than the other types of kuhlis, and the body has a more slippery or "slimy" texture. It has ten to 14 long, broad, quadrangular black bars that nearly encircle the body on an orange background. The bars never have a pale inner zone. The caudal fin is black or has a large black base blotch and a sub terminal black bar or row of spots. *P. myersi* is very similar in color to *P. kuhlii* and *P. semicincta*. This loach requires an omnivorous diet with a wide variety of foods including flake and frozen foods. Favorites include bloodworms, brine shrimp, and sinking algae wafers. Keep in groups of three or more. *Pangio myersi* can reach a maximum size of 4 inches (10 cm).

Pangio myersi.

Pangio oblonga
(Valenciennes, 1846)

Synonyms: *Acanthophthalmus javanicus, Pangio javanicus*

Common Names: Java loach, black kuhli, chocolate kuhli, panga (Bengali)

Distribution: Indochina, Java, Sumatra, Borneo and Malay Peninsula. Reported from India and Bangladesh.

Occurrences: Mekong River Basin, Laos/Cambodia/Thailand/Vietnam
Chao Phraya River Basin, Thailand
Nan River, Thailand
Seroke Stream, India
Darjiling River, India
Dangtong River, Cambodia
Sungai Pinoh River, Borneo, Indonesia
Brang River, Malaysia
Tersat River, Malaysia
Mandalay Division, Myanmar
Tenasserim Division, Myanmar

Habitat: found on the bottom in sluggish parts of rapidly flowing streams with a sandy substrate.

Ideal Tank Parameters: pH: 6.2 to 7.0; Temp 76° to 82°F (24° to 28°C)

Pangio oblonga

This is one of the "un-banded" kuhlis. The fish is uniform in color, ranging from a reddish-brown or milk chocolate to almost black. The fins are translucent, and the belly tends to be slightly paler than the rest of the body. This loach requires a varied diet including flake and frozen foods. Favorites include bloodworms, brine shrimp, and sinking algae wafers. Keep in groups of three or more. *Pangio oblonga* reaches a maximum size of 3.125 inches (8 cm). This species has been bred in aquaria.

Pangio oblonga.

Pangio pangia
(Hamilton, 1822)

Synonyms: *Acanthophthalmus pangia, Pangio pangio, Pangio cinnamomea*

Common Names: cinnamon loach

Distribution: India, Bangladesh, and Myanmar

Occurrences: Mitkyina District, Myanmar Sagaing Division, Myanmar

Habitat: inhabits slow-moving rivers with a sandy bottom

Ideal Tank Parameters: pH: 6.4 to 7.0; Temp 77° to 80°F (25° to 26°C)

Pangio pangia

An "un-banded" kuhli, this fish is a uniform pinkish-tan color. The fins are translucent, and the belly is slightly paler than the rest of the body and has a golden hue. Feed as you would other species of *Pangio* and keep in groups of three or more. *P. pangia* reaches a maximum size of 3.125 inches (8 cm).

Pangio semicincta

A highly variable species, *Pangio semicincta* has nine to 12 black bars across the back over a reddish-orange background. There are two or three bars at the head and one or two bars circling the body at the tail. The rest of the

Pangio pangia.

Pangio semicincta
(Fraser-Brunner, 1940)

Synonyms: *Acanthophthalmus semicinctus, Pangio semicinctus*

Common Names: half-banded loach

Distribution: Malay Peninsula, Borneo and Sumatra

Occurrences: Kapuas River, Borneo, Indonesia
Sungai River tributaries, Malaysia
Pahang River Basin, Malaysia
Medan, Sumatra, Indonesia
Baleh River, Sarawak, Borneo, Malaysia
Lake Chin Chin Jasin, Malacca, Malaysia
Nerus River, Malaysia
Sungei Selectar River, Singapore

Habitat: lives on the bottom of sandy or muddy creeks and streams among leaf litter or heavy vegetation. Prefers warmer waters

Ideal Tank Parameters: pH: 6.2 to 6.8; Temp 78° to 85° F (25.5° to 29°C)

Pangio semicincta.

bars run from the back down to the midline. The bars tend to be uneven, sometimes connecting to form a solid wedge of black joining at the base to form a saddle pattern. Females have smaller fins; males have a thickened second pectoral ray. The fish previously called *P. kuhlii* from the Malay Peninsula, Sumatra, and Borneo is now recognized as *P. semicincta*. In Singapore this fish is regarded as being a locally endangered species. This loach should be fed as with other kuhlis and kept in

Loaches

groups of three or more. *P. semicincta* reaches a maximum size of 4 inches (10 cm).

Pangio shelfordii

This kuhli is distinguished by its color pattern consisting of a mid-lateral series of irregular blotches, sometimes forming a mid-lateral stripe. Its back is finely mottled with a median row of large black saddles or a similar pattern over a yellow-pink background. There is a vertical black blotch at the caudal base, and the tail fin itself is mottled. This is one of the cool-water kuhlis and will begin to experience discomfort at temperatures of 79°F (26°C) or higher.

This omnivorous kuhli requires a diet with a wide variety of foods including flake and frozen foods. Favorites include bloodworms, brine shrimp, and sinking algae wafers. *Pangio shelfordii* should be kept in groups of three or more. This fish reaches a maximum size of 3.125 inches (8 cm). It is considered a locally endangered species in Singapore.

Pangio shelfordii
(Popta, 1903)

Synonyms: *Acanthophthalmus shelfordi, Acanthophthalmus muraeniformis*

Common Names: Borneo loach, Shelford's loach, spotted eel loach, spotted kuhli loach

Distribution: Southern Malay Peninsula, Sumatra, and Borneo

Occurrences: Kapuas River Basin, Borneo, Indonesia
Mahakam River Basin, Borneo, Indonesia
Sungai Selectar River, Singapore
Sedili Besar River, Malaysia

Habitat: found in cooler brown or slightly black waters, usually among leaf litter

Ideal Tank Parameters: pH: 6.0 to 6.5; Temp 72° to 77°F (22-25°C)

Pangio shelfordii.

Weather Loaches, Long-Nosed Loaches, and Other Oddballs

Of all the species of loaches from the family Cobitidae, the kuhli loaches remain the most popular and available to the aquarium trade. However, other species find their way into many loach keepers' tanks from time to time, and these loaches will be discussed in the following pages. The species included were chosen based on their popularity and other outstanding characteristics that really do make them unique specimens for the home aquarium.

> **But What's in a Name?**
>
> Acantopsis choirorhynchus *may be the horseface loach, but breaking down the scientific Latin name reveals that it is actually named after another animal: acantha (sting) plus opsis (view; eye) and choiros (pig) plus rhynchus (snout).Therefore the name means "sting-eye, pig-snout."*

Acantopsis choirorhynchus

One of the burrowing loaches, in the blink of an eye *Acantopsis choirorhynchus* can disappear into the substrate, where it spends most of its time unseen. Occasionally it pushes up to the surface, just enough to allow the aquarist to see a pair of little beady eyes staring back. This loach tends to be rather skittish and will jump out of the tank when startled, so care should be taken to ensure that the tank lid is tight-fitting and secure. A tank with a small gravel substrate will do, but these fish prefer sand, which minimizes stress by making them feel more secure. *A. choirorhynchus* is most active at

The horseface loach *Acantopsis choirorhynchus* is most happy hiding in the tank's substrate.

Acantopsis choirorhynchus
(Bleeker, 1854)

Synonyms: *Cobitis choirorhynchus*

Common Names: horsehead loach, horseface loach, pa it (Laotian), ca chia voi (Vietnamese), pla chon sai (Thai), pla kluay (Thai), jeler (Malay)

Distribution: South Asia, from India to Vietnam. Also Borneo, Sumatra, and Java

Occurrences: Irrawaddy River Basin, Myanmar
Chao Phraya River Basin, Thailand
Mekong River Basin, Thailand/Laos/Cambodia/Vietnam
Kapuas River Basin, Kalimantan Barat, Borneo, Indonesia
Hari River, Sumatra, Indonesia
Trengganu River, Malaysia
Tembeling River, Malaysia
Muar River, Malaysia
Tersat River, Malaysia
Patani River, Malaysia

Habitat: clear streams and rivers with moderate water flow and sandy substrate

Ideal Tank Parameters: pH 6.4 to 7.4; Temp 77° to 81°F (25° to 27°C)

bending downward about halfway between eyes and mouth. This species has three pairs of barbels, two below and one smaller pair above the mouth. It has an elongated light tan body with 14 to 16 brown saddle-shaped markings on its back that run the length of the fish. There is a row of 14 to 16 similarly colored dots that run the length of the fish along the lateral line. In some individuals these dots occur over a lightly speckled background. The fins are clear with golden highlights, and the tail is clear with several rows of faint vertical spots. *A. choirorhynchus* reaches a maximum size of nearly 8 inches (20 cm) in length, but is considered mature from 2.4 inches (6 cm).

The horseface loach should be offered an omnivorous diet. It particularly likes small live or frozen foods like bloodworms, brine shrimp, and daphnia, and it will readily accept flake food.

The ever-watchful eye of the burrowing horseface loach. The horseface loach is often confused with a similar-looking member of its genus, the long-nosed loach (*A. octoactinotos*). The long-nosed loach can be distinguished from the horseface by its straight facial profile, slower movements, and more aggressive behavior toward smaller fishes.

night and when not buried in substrate it can often be spotted lounging on the surface of the sand.

The horseface loach gets its name from its distinctive head, which resembles that of a horse. The eyes are closely set high atop the head, parallel with the gill openings. The nose is long and thin,

Cobitis taenia taenia

This temperate loach holds the prize for geographic diversity. The spined loach occurs in rivers from the Seine to the Volga, across Europe including Great Britain and on into Asia, in cool waters of areas that experience winter conditions. It inhabits both clear lakes and running waters. Various subspecies are known and identified, but all the spined loaches of Britain and Europe are true *Cobitis taenia taenia*. Although widespread, individual populations tend to be isolated from one another. The survival of the species in certain parts of Europe is threatened by human activity, particularly channelization of rivers and the removal of macrophytes (vascular water plants) from the unshaded parts of rivers. Studies have shown that the species' occurrence seems to be tightly tied to the presence of sandy areas of substrate with close proximity to water plants. Artificial removal of water plants or dredging from its rivers for navigation purposes causes habitat loss and reduces oxygen levels within the substrate. This can have an effect on the percentage of eggs hatching. As such, it is considered a threatened species and listed under Appendix 3 of the Bern Convention and Appendix II of the EC Directive on conservation of natural habitats for flora and fauna.

C. taenia taenia grows to a length of 5.25 inches (13.5 cm). Its elongated body is variable in color but may be yellowish-gray along the back, fading to delicate gray or dull yellow on the flanks. The belly is pale to white. The back and sides are mottled with fine brown spots. There is a row of brown spots along the back from head to tail, with a row of intense dark spots to either side of it. Below the mid-line of the sides there is another row of pale-edged brown spots. A vertical black stripe is present at the root of the caudal fin. The fins are pale gray to clear, and sometimes the

Cobitis taenia taenia
(Linnaeus, 1758)

Synonyms: *Cobitis spilura, Cobitis taenia dalmatina, Cobitis taenia danubialis, Cobitis taenia narentana, Cobitis taenia ohridana, Cobitis taenioides*

Common Names: spined loach, spiny loach

Distribution: widespread and common across Europe and northern Asia: in the UK, in England but not in Wales or Scotland; Iberian Peninsula in the west to northern Russia, Japan and Taiwan in the east; and southern parts of Scandinavia in the north to Iran in the south

Habitat: slow-moving or still waters in streams with sandy substrate and patches of water plants

Ideal Tank Parameters: pH 7.0 to 7.7; Temp 57.2° to 64.4°F (14° to 18°C), colder during winter

dorsal and caudal fins have rows of spots. The eye may be silvery, gold, or orange in color. The suborbital spine has a forked tip. If the water the fish are living in suffers oxygen depletion at any time, they can use the gut for supplementary breathing, gulping air at the surface and expelling it from the anus.

This largely nocturnal loach should be kept in a tank with subdued lighting. It absolutely must have a substrate of fine sand, since it spends much time burrowing. *C. taenia taenia* is generally solitary in

Cobitis taenia taenia.

Loaches

Alias

Due to its wide distribution, *Cobitis taenia taenia* has numerous regional names. They include: loche de rivere (France), steinbeisser / dom grundel (Germany), kleine modderkruiper (Holland), cobite comune / cobite fluviale (Italy), colmilleja (Spain), serpentina (Portugal), plz obycajny / sekavec obecny (Czechoslovakia), svirluga / zvirluga (Romania), vago csik (Hungary), vinos (Greece), kozka (Poland), shtschipovka (Russia), pig smerling (Denmark), nissoga (Sweden), sand smett (Norway), eojuskrioill (Iceland), rantaneula (Finland), lakh mukhattat (Arabic), zagafgaziya iliskani (Azerbaijan), mahi roshtegar or roftegar (Khuzestan), and tairiku-shima-dojo (Japan).

nature and prefers to remain buried in either sand, mud that is not too thick, or dense weed growths. When the fish is concealed, the body is bent into a concave arch so that only the head and tail protrude. This loach swims by using undulating motions over short distances.

The German name "steinbeisser" (rendered in German works as "Steinbeisser," since written German capitalizes all names) means "stone-biter" and refers to its method of eating. The diet of the spined loach consists of small crustaceans such as ostracods, copepods, and rotifers found in the substrate. A mouthful of mud or sand is taken in and chewed food items are extracted, and the residue is expelled through the gill openings. In captivity they will eat most foods, but frozen and live foods are favorites.

The pectoral fins are used as a method of sexing this species. In the male, the second ray is thickened and there is a prominently enlarged scale at its base. This is known as the Canastreni scale. The female's pectoral rays are all of equal thickness.

In the wild, spawning occurs April to June, among plant matter or submerged roots. The fish will seek out slower-flowing or still water. The eggs are shed indiscriminately and are non-adhesive. The spined loach is a fractional spawner, releasing batches of 14 to 18 eggs at intervals over a period up to 23 days. The total number of eggs per female can be over 4,000 during a single reproductive season. The eggs are quite large at approximately 0.09 inches (2.5 mm) in diameter. At a temperature of 59°F (15°C), eggs will hatch after six to ten days. Total larval length is around 0.19 inches (5 mm) at hatching. The young are easily raised in an established tank because the fry will feed on microorganisms they find in the substrate.

The species has been bred in aquaria, but this will occur only after a cold overwintering. Indeed, temperature is a critical factor with this species. Fish acclimatized to aquarium conditions can tolerate 64.4°F (18°C), but freshly caught wild fish must be kept in considerably colder water. Sexual maturity seems to be attained at about two years, and the fish live about five years in aquaria.

Lepidocephalichthys guntea

Lepidocephalichthys guntea is an attractively marked elongate loach similar in general appearance to *C. taenia taenia* and the *Misgurnus* species. It is characterized by its tan body color and dark broken horizontal bars running the length of its body. Male specimens have a bony spine in the pectoral fins; this spine is absent in females.

This species is generally a very peaceful and sometimes timid fish. Even though it may reach

Lepidocephalicthys guntea
(Hamilton, 1822)

Synonyms: *Cobitis guntea,*
Lepidocephlus guntea

Common names: peppered loach,
panther loach, peppered dojo,
guntea loach, goira (Nepali),
nakata (Nepali), gutum (Bengali),
mori (Marathi), ngakijrou
(Manipuri)

Distribution: Pakistan to Thailand

Occurrences: Bagmati River Basin
and Chitawan Valley, Nepal
Kali Gandaki River, Nepal
Indus River, Pakistan
Salane River, India
Chilka Lake, India
West Bengal, India
Ganges River Basin,
India/Bangladesh
Brahmaputra River Basin, India
Salween River Basin,
Myanmar/Thailand

Habitat: low and clear standing
water

Ideal Tank Parameters: pH 6.8 to
7.6; Temp 70° to 78°F (21.1° to
25.5°C)

ranging from a river tank to a more traditional tropical aquarium. Clean, well-oxygenated water with some current is preferred. Temperatures should range from the typical tropical range to slightly below. Plenty of hiding places should be provided for this shy species as well as a smooth sand or gravel substrate for burrowing.

In captivity the peppered loach will enjoy a wide variety of live, frozen, and prepared foods. Bloodworms, brine shrimp, pellets, and flakes are all readily accepted.

Lepidocephalichthys guntea.

nearly 6 inches (15 cm) and grow rather thick in girth, it may still be chased away from food by more aggressive smaller fishes. As with many other loach species, it tends to become more reclusive as it matures and is most active in low light conditions.

Lepidocephalichthys guntea can be kept in a wide variety of conditions. It will live well in tank setups

Misgurnus anguillicaudatus

The weather loach and its cousin *Misgurnus mizolepis* are named because of their sensitivity to changes in barometric pressure. The swim bladder in both species is reduced to a size at which it has lost its hydrostatic function and has become a sensory organ. Its outer exposed surface is connected with the skin through a channel between the bands of muscle, conveying thermo-barometrical impressions to the auditory nerves.

During major changes in the weather, these fish become agitated and may dart about the tank. Like many other members of the family Cobitidae, the weather loach is able to literally swallow air at the surface and absorb the oxygen through a membrane in the gut. Unused oxygen is then passed out through the anus of the fish. The efficiency of this breathing method and the durability of this fish is such that individuals have been discovered living in burrows in damp mud with no water present.

Adult male specimens of *M. anguillicaudatus* have broader pectoral fins when viewed from above, and the females generally have fuller abdomens. The fish is a golden brown color mottled by darker gray-green or brown spots, with the belly being paler or almost white. Five pairs of barbels are present; the suborbital spines are difficult to detect when hidden beneath the skin.

In their natural habitat, these fish spawn during the monsoon season when fields and rice paddies become flooded.

Misgurnus anguillicaudatus
(Cantor, 1842)

Synonyms: *Cobitis anguillicaudata, Misgurnus crossochilus, Misgurnus lividus, Ussuria leptocephala, Misgurnus fossilis anguillicaudatus*

Common Names: weather loach, oriental weather fish, dojo loach, pond loach, ca diet (Khmer), dojo (Japanese), nai chau (Cantonese), vostochnyi (Russian)

Distribution: China, Laos, Cambodia, Thailand, Vietnam, Myanmar, Taiwan, Hong Kong, South Korea (and probably North Korea too), Japan. Introduced into the United States, Australia, Philippine Islands, Palau, and Turkmenistan

Occurrences: Mekong River Basin, Indochina
Yangtze River Basin, China
Xi Jiang River Basin, China
Tarim River Basin, China
Tugur River Basin, China
Amur River Basin, China
Liao River south to Guangzhou, China
Kwangtung Province, China
Yunnan Province, Hainan, China
Sedanka River near Vladivostok, Russia
Tumen-Ula River, North Korea
Hokkaido and Kyushu in Japan
Irrawaddy River, Myanmar
Tonkin and Annam provinces of northern Vietnam
Taiwan (probably introduced)

Habitat: rivers, lakes, ponds, rice paddies, etc., with muddy substrate and ample plant matter. Inhabits depths of up to 16.5 feet (5 m)

Ideal Tank Parameters: pH 7.0 to 8.0; Temp 50° to 68°F (10° to 20°C)

Misgurnus anguillicaudatus.

Loaches

The Hazard of Weather Loaches

Because this species is cultivated for human consumption and used as a bait fish, there have been numerous escapes from fish farms along with unscrupulous releases by irresponsible fish keepers. This has led to the establishment of breeding populations which have had a negative effect upon the local fish fauna due to unnatural competition.

In North America, this fish is established in several flood-control channels in Huntington Beach and Westminster in Orange County, California, as well as in the headwaters of the Shiawassee River in Oakland County, Michigan. Imported as an aquarium fish since at least the late 1930s, the weather loach is believed to have escaped from an aquarium fish cultivation facility in Westminster, California.

Because of their ability to endure both temperate and subtropical conditions, they have become invasive in areas like Hawaii, where they were introduced before 1900. They can be found in streams in Kauai, Maui, and Oahu.

Weather loaches have been declared a noxious species in Queensland, Australia. For this reason it is illegal to possess, rear, sell, or buy weather loaches there. Offenders face large penalties. There have been isolated reports of this species living in Queensland waters, plus New South Wales, the Australian Capital Territory, and Victoria.

In England, weather loaches are on a list of prohibited species, requiring a license to sell or own them. However, the particular species of weather loach listed in the prohibition is *M. fossilis*, a European species. The species most commonly sold is *M. anguillicaudatus*, which is imported from China and is considered to be a "warm water" species, is not currently covered by the legislation.

Weather loaches are sexually mature at around 4 inches (10 cm). The male wraps his body around the female, which triggers her to release a cloud of eggs that are fertilized during the process. Eggs are left unattended amid the substrate. While these loaches rarely breed in captivity, instances have been recorded.

This is a very peaceful loach and an excellent bottom cleaner. They have been recommended for the removal of snail populations and will work well to this end. At an adult length of 9.75 inches (24.8 cm), *M. anguillicaudatus* makes an excellent addition to aquaria with large surface areas of substrate. They are known to enjoy burrowing, so areas of rounded soft sand are recommended. Weather loaches are tolerant of a wide range of water conditions and have been successfully kept in outdoor ponds as far north as Canada and the northwestern United States.

Weather loaches enjoy a varied diet of flake and frozen foods, and fresh worms, crustaceans, and other invertebrates and their larvae are taken readily.

Somileptus gongota

Probably one of the most unusual-looking loaches, *Somileptus gongota* has a face only a mother could love. The head of this burrowing loach is disproportionately large for its long, tapered body, usually accounting for nearly 20 percent of the animal's total length. *S. gongota* has six barbels surrounding a small down-turned mouth with which it sucks up sand. The sand is then expelled through the gills, the fish retaining only the edible morsels. In its wake are patterns in the substrate that resemble a Japanese sand garden. This feeding behavior means that a sand substrate is absolutely essential for *S. gongota* to survive in the home aquarium.

The mooseface loach is a shy, nocturnal fish and an exceedingly reserved feeder. If forced to compete with other fish for food it will slowly starve to death. Newly acquired fish may at first accept only small live or frozen foods such as daphnia and brine shrimp. Once settled in, they will learn to relish high-quality flake food, but daphnia or brine shrimp should be fed a few times a week to keep them in good condition. A healthy, well-fed mooseface loach should have a smoothly tapered body. An abrupt thinning of the body beginning behind the gills is indicative of a poorly nourished fish.

Though not a schooling fish, the mooseface loach does enjoy the company of its own kind and should be kept in groups of two or more. Good tankmates

The mooseface loach, beautiful in its own way.

Somileptus gongota
(Hamilton, 1822)

Synonyms: *Somileptes gongota,
Cobitis gongota*

Common Names: mooseface loach,
moosehead loach, moose-faced
loach, gongota loach, poia
(Bengali), gora gutum (Bengali)

Distribution: India, Bangladesh,
and Nepal

Occurrences: Kushiara River,
Bangladesh
Ganges River Basin,
India/Bangladesh
Brahmaputra River Basin, India
Sessa River, India
Tista River Basin,
India/Bangladesh

Habitat: shallows of slow-moving
streams with sandy or muddy
substrate

Ideal Tank Parameters: pH 6.4 to
7.4; Temp 77° to 81°F (25° to 27°C)

include similar species such as the horseface or kuhli loaches and peaceful tetras.

Given its unassuming nature, *S. gongota*'s only defense mechanisms are its outstanding camouflage and its ability to vanish beneath the sand with lightning speed. At times the mooseface loach can be a little skittish and in its haste to flee may leap from the aquarium. A secure cover is a must.

S. gongota's eyes are set high atop the head, allowing the fish to lie completely buried with only its eyes peering above the surface, scanning for predators. As with most other loaches, the mooseface has a suborbital spine, although that spine it is very short and rarely displayed. The fish is a mottled charcoal to light gray in color, with an irregular black band undulating along the midline giving the appearance of six to eight saddles across the back. If viewed from above, the pattern looks like the substrate of a sandy stream, rendering the fish nearly invisible. The belly of *S. gongota* is white with opaque, lightly speckled pectoral, pelvic, and anal fins. The dorsal fin and tail are usually kept folded and have the same mottled coloration as the rest of the body. The species reaches an adult length of 5 inches (13 cm).

Chapter 9

The Family
Balitoridae

The rivers of Southeast Asia consist of a variety of environments to which loaches have adapted over millions of years. The high, fast-flowing streams feeding into the mighty lowland rivers are the biggest challenge in those environments, requiring highly specialized adaptations for fishes to thrive there.

Water Conditions and Diet

The streams inhabited by fishes of the family Balitoridae tend to be relatively shallow and may be as little as 3 feet (1 m) wide, with water speeds as high as 10 feet (3 m) per second. They share the habitat with other families of fishes, predominately cyprinids, in the lower flow areas, but above 2,000 feet (600 m) in altitude balitorids become the dominant fishes; they can still be found at 6,000 feet (1,800 m)!

These are places of generally cooler water, 68° to 78.8°F (20° to 26°C). It is higher in oxygen content (over 8 mg/L), but lower in nutrients than at lower altitudes. The pH is typically between 7 and 8, and often the water is hard due to its flow over calciferous rocks. The high-speed current caused by incline and by having the water forced past boulders and other obstacles creates tremendous

Gastromyzon ocellatus. Generally species with more highly adapted, dorso-ventrally compressed shapes will live in the higher flow areas, relying on algae for the major part of their diet. They have mouths developed for rasping algae from rocks.

The Threat of Logging

Because of their algal diet, many of the balitorids are at risk from excessive logging operations being carried out in some of their home countries (Borneo, Myanmar). The disturbance of the ground leads to having large amounts of debris being washed into the rivers. This can lift sedimentation into the water column, which eventually settles and covers the fishes' food source. Over time, the water will remove this sediment, but it can take time for balitorid stocks to recover.

mixing of water and air, resulting in high oxygen levels. The rapid flow also creates an environment that prevents normal levels of organic debris from settling. Only at slower water velocity, in areas of greater width and with deeper pools, can detritus settle to be utilized for survival. Aquatic plants generally do not survive the high current.

In some areas the streams may be almost covered by the forest canopy, but in others they are fully exposed to the sun's harsh glare, creating excellent conditions for algal growth on rocks and boulders that make up the stream substrate. Living within the algae are multiple species of small invertebrates that are also eaten. Utilizing such food sources, as many hillstream loaches do, requires special adaptations in order to live and procreate successfully.

The family Balitoridae consists of many genera of fishes with physical adaptations ranging from flattened sucker-bodied shape to those of the torpedo-shaped bodies. These adaptations help the fishes survive the various effects caused by moving waters, mainly drag and lift.

Drag and Lift

Any moving object, whether it moves through a gas or a liquid, creates drag. Drag is defined as aerodynamic resistance of the object through the water. Drag is generated by the difference in velocity of the fish and the water. It makes no difference whether the fish moves through the water or the water moves past the fish; drag will still be generated. The more smoothly the water passes over the fish, the less drag will be created. A shape with a very low drag coefficient is a sphere with a cone on the side that the air departs (i.e., a teardrop shape).

Then there is lift. Lift is created when the water flowing over the fish has to travel farther than the water flowing under the fish. This creates lower pressure above, inducing lift. The fish can use this as a method of vertical movement that consumes very little energy.

Movement in Water

Water is an inherently heavy substance to move through. Most humans know how difficult it is to run through chest-deep, even waist-high or knee-deep, water. Movement requires energy, and the easier it is for an organism to move through liquid or air the less energy is required for movement.

For a fish that lives in fast-flowing water, movement isn't a problem. Once in the water flow no energy is required, apart from a minimal steering effort. The problem in a stream is staying still, especially if the main food source is growing on the rocks.

Profile Drag

Another component of drag is known as profile drag. This relates to the shape of an object. The thickness of an aircraft's wing relative to its width is known as its chord. This affects its lifting capability. A thick chord, like that of a Boeing 747, creates the huge lift needed to get the monster off the ground, but it also generates increased drag. In comparison, a jet fighter is thinner and creates less lift. This is why fighter aircraft, though lighter in weight, require greater take-off speeds and create less drag. Therefore, a fish that has less chord will create less lift and less drag. A by-product of the increased body area is that the effective suction induced by the fin "pumps" of sucker type hillstream loaches will be increased, and the fish's potential for staying put in even faster water is improved.

Induced Drag

Induced drag is also present in aircraft. This occurs at the wingtips, by the meeting of low- and high-pressure areas. Vortices form, contributing to greater drag by creating turbulence behind the aircraft. This is why large aircraft, with their deep chord wings, require large separation distances on airport approaches. Their "wake" disturbs the air that much. The geometry of the wing (its relationship of length to chord) affects induced drag. A long, thin wing creates less induced drag; accordingly, a fish with thin chord and wide fins would also have less induced drag.

Gastromyzon ocellatus.

Almost without exception, the more highly adapted species will tend to sit upon a surface with the dorsal fin lowered and caudal fin folded. This further decreases drag over the back and allows water to leave the rear of the fish with minimal turbulence. These fishes open the fins only when making fast moves or displaying to one another. All these physiological adaptations create a fish that can stay exactly where it chooses, with little expense of energy.

> *Comparing one species to another, it is apparent that the fishes with un-joined fins have a slightly more rounded body cross-section, while the fishes with the joined, full-sucker type of fins are more laterally compressed to varying degrees.*

How These Physical Adaptations Work

There is a logical reasoning behind the various extremes of fin adaptation in the subfamily Balitorinae. Such species as *Homaloptera* have enlarged pectoral fins that these loaches use like race-car spoilers to force themselves down against a surface. The more highly adapted species get called sucker-belly loaches (among other names discussed later in this chapter), for a good reason. If the flow of water under the fish can be reduced, the pressure differential that causes lift is largely eliminated. Resistance to movement, then, comes

Oxygen Requirements

Although the sucker-type fishes use their special abilities most of the time, they are not what one could call sedentary. They are lively and will shuffle around like little clockwork toys for the majority of the day searching for food and grazing on the rocks. They can, when it is necessary, move with amazing speed. It seems that they are gifted with explosive energy good for the short bursts that may be needed in nature to move in the fast water flow or to evade predators. When observing these fishes in a dealer's tank, they will often not move around much, giving a false impression of being somewhat boring as an ornamental species for the home aquarium. There is a reason for this lack of movement.

All fishes require oxygen, but in the case of hillstream loaches their oxygen requirements are much higher than the majority of other aquarium-kept species. Their natural environments are so high in oxygen saturation that the fishes have blood hemoglobin with a low affinity to oxygen. This creates an inability on the part of the fishes to breathe effectively in the lower concentrations of oxygen found in most aquaria. Due to their high oxygen requirements and specialized adaptations to the extremes of water flow found in their natural habitat, the aquarist will never see the unique behaviors of these fishes unless a specialized tank setup is used (see Chapter 2). In the dealer's tank these loaches are unsettled, with minimal cover for security, and may be suffering from oxygen deprivation, which over time can be detrimental to their health.

Loaches

down to the weight of the fish plus its friction against the resting surface versus the drag of its body and the speed of the water. One way to increase the resistance to movement is to create negative pressure under the body, thereby effectively increasing the body weight and its resistance to movement.

Some of the species (*Protomyzon*) have enlarged fins that allow them to shut out the under-flow, while others (*Pseudogastromyzon*) have pectoral and pelvic fins that overlap and create a larger shut-off area. Some species (*Sinogastromyzon*) have the pelvic fins joined together underneath the rear of the fish, further increasing the sucker effect. In the fishes with overlapping fins, some species have the upper rear portion of the pectoral fins modified into a flap, which the fish can move and appear to pump out water from between its belly and the resting surface. When the fish shuts off the "valve," the fins seal the fish to the surface and resist the body drag.

Evolution

The highly flattened species may live in faster streams than the less specifically adapted ones. Of course, the evolution of a species is not actually driven by it adapting to a given environment; rather, successive generations include members who have certain differences that allow them to better utilize a given ecological niche. The various species of these fishes changed and diversified, possibly from a common ancestor, into those we see today. The way they evolved allowed them to live in a particular part of a fast-flowing river, and their degree of shape difference allows some to live in the strongest currents while others might be swept away. This enables them to keep themselves clamped to rocks and utilize the food sources available in those locations. Indeed, collection

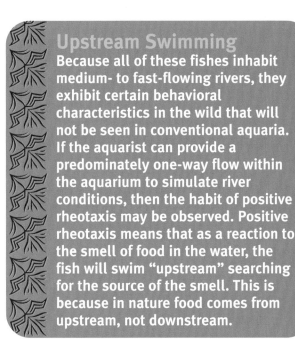

Upstream Swimming
Because all of these fishes inhabit medium- to fast-flowing rivers, they exhibit certain behavioral characteristics in the wild that will not be seen in conventional aquaria. If the aquarist can provide a predominately one-way flow within the aquarium to simulate river conditions, then the habit of positive rheotaxis may be observed. Positive rheotaxis means that as a reaction to the smell of food in the water, the fish will swim "upstream" searching for the source of the smell. This is because in nature food comes from upstream, not downstream.

expeditions in the wild have shown extreme localization of species. Certain species inhabit particular environments, and generally this is governed by the speed of water flow.

Territorial Spats

Because the family Balitoridae contains so many diverse species, there are differences in behavior in the aquarium environment. Generally these fishes are somewhat territorial, but they do not do serious damage to one another during any skirmishes. Some *Schistura* and similar species can be quite feisty, but these specific cases will be discussed in their species descriptions (see Chapter 10).

With most of the sucker-belly type balitorids, territorial disputes are normally resolved by short skirmishes, but sometimes quite prolonged trials of strength can ensue. These often take the form of "king of the castle" type interactions where one fish pushes or swims over another in an attempt to cover its opponent.

Being "on top" literally seems to be the goal in these battles. All the rapid movements involved in the interaction are accompanied by frantic flapping of the pectoral fins and the spreading of the dorsal and caudal fins, often displaying bright colors in some species. This is likely one reason that the name "butterfly" is so often associated with these fishes in the ornamental fish trade. Aggression in *Schistura* species can be more violent, with vicious tail-slapping and some biting being observed.

The Sucker-Body Hillstream Loaches

Fishes of the family Balitoridae first entered the aquarium hobby in the mid 1990s. Hobbyists often became frustrated because these fishes would survive for only a very short time. Nobody really understood their requirements. They were exported from countries in Southeast Asia to aquariums all over the world and given confusing trade names such as Hong Kong plecos because of their superficial resemblance to the *Plecostomus* species.

Two male *Sewellia lineolata* engaged in a territorial dispute. These fights may be brief or carry on for extended periods. They consist of pushing, tail slapping, and trying a "topping" maneuver as shown here. One will try to get on top of the other, probably as a sign of dominance.

Plecostomus (South American catfishes of the family Loricariidae) live quite happily in regular aquaria, but the high oxygen content required by hillstream loaches is not normally met under these conditions.

Due to the persistence of hobbyists, many of the secrets of meeting hillstream loaches' needs in aquaria have been unlocked, and some species have now even been bred in captivity. Positive identification of species being imported is still almost non-existent, because the export trade still lists the fishes variously as Hong Kong plecos, Chinese butterfly loaches, Borneo suckers, sucker-belly loaches, and multiple other names, depending on their country of origin.

Another common trade name is lizard fish, which seems to be a catchall name for the various *Homaloptera* species. At the retail level, few fish shops actually bother to positively identify the fishes or instruct customers as to their specialized requirements. This is often because fish shop personnel themselves are not aware that these fishes require special care.

The sections that follow make identifications of known species clearer for those loaches that are more regularly imported. However, one thing that makes the hobby interesting for enthusiasts of these endearing fishes is that frequently within shipments there are contaminants of other species, often previously unseen in the hobby. Collecting and identifying these "oddballs" is a hobby in itself. Positive identification of these species is complicated by the paucity of photographic record available, though some species are described in scientific nomenclature.

Family Balitoridae—Sucker-Body Hillstream Loaches

Beaufortia kweichowensis

This is probably the most widely exported species of this group and the one most likely to be found at the local fish store. Although not brightly colored, its unusual shape and fluttering mode of travel make it an attractive aquarium inhabitant. A somewhat more retiring species than others, it will, however, become more intrepid given plenty of hiding places. The inclusion of some lively top and middle-swimming dither fishes also makes them bolder.

In a mixed community of hillstream loaches, this species will usually be the one that ultimately wins territorial skirmishes. Individuals are often imported at larger sizes than other species and can grow to 3.9 inches (10 cm), so their bulk determines their dominance. However, despite this, they are not an aggressive species. None of their fights result

Beaufortia kweichowensis
(Fang, 1931)

Synonyms: *Gastromyzon leveretti kweichowensis*

Common Names: butterfly hillstream loach, Hong Kong pleco, Chinese sucker

Distribution: widespread in China

Occurrences: San-ho Hsien, Kweichow, China

Habitat: highland streams; fast-flowing water over boulders

Ideal Tank Parameters: pH 7.0 to 8.0; Temp 68° to 75°F (20° to 23.8°C)

Sometimes sold as the Chinese butterfly loach, *Beaufortia kweichowensis* is relatively common, and makes a great addition to the river tank.

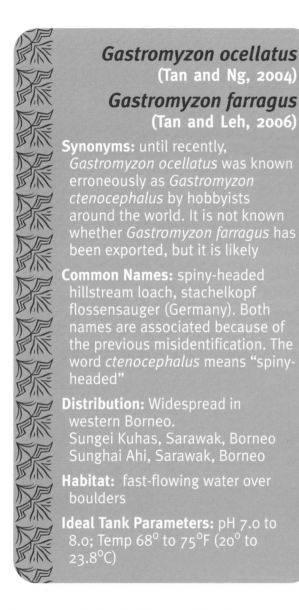

Gastromyzon ocellatus
(Tan and Ng, 2004)
Gastromyzon farragus
(Tan and Leh, 2006)

Synonyms: until recently, *Gastromyzon ocellatus* was known erroneously as *Gastromyzon ctenocephalus* by hobbyists around the world. It is not known whether *Gastromyzon farragus* has been exported, but it is likely

Common Names: spiny-headed hillstream loach, stachelkopf flossensauger (Germany). Both names are associated because of the previous misidentification. The word *ctenocephalus* means "spiny-headed"

Distribution: Widespread in western Borneo.
Sungei Kuhas, Sarawak, Borneo
Sunghai Ahi, Sarawak, Borneo

Habitat: fast-flowing water over boulders

Ideal Tank Parameters: pH 7.0 to 8.0; Temp 68° to 75°F (20° to 23.8°C)

pellets, algae wafers, frozen bloodworms, and brine shrimp. Blanched spinach and kale leaves provide additional vegetable matter.

Gastromyzon ocellatus and G. farragus

These attractively marked loaches are an asset to any tank that meets their requirements. One unique aspect of their markings is that the broad bands across their backs have soft, blurred edges, creating an illusion of their being out of focus with the rest of the fish. In *Gastromyzon ocellatus*, the tail is marked with red on the dorsal and ventral margins. The center is blue to purple, with some fine black striping, creating a very beautiful display during the infrequent times these fish open their fins.

G. ocellatus is easily identified by the occelli markings on the rear half of the body sides. *G. farragus* lacks these and has an irregular distribution of small spots. The paler stripes on the back are also thinner compared with those of *G. ocellatus*.

Imports are irregular, and often these fish come mixed in with other hillstream species. They appear to be more sociable than other species of the sucker-belly loaches, often sitting around in groups, yet they will still indulge in typical displays to one another over territorial issues. Females are probably plumper with a back profile that is more curved than that of a male, but there are no obvious sexual differences. They have not been bred in aquaria.

G. ocellatus has definitely been exported and appears irregularly for sale. It is unknown whether *G. farragus* has reached the hobby, but it is possible, because it is collected in the same streams as *G. scitulus*.

Both species reach around 2 inches (5 cm) in length. Feeding in aquaria is similar to that for other hillstream species. They are active most of the day, constantly grazing the rocks and aquarium glass for algae and other food.

in any actual physical damage. They have never bred in aquaria and are very difficult to sex, but males appear to be brighter in coloring than females and are usually more forthright in territorial defense.

Beaufortia kweichowensis eats small aquatic invertebrates living within the algae they graze on rocks. In aquaria, they eat flake foods, sinking

Gastromyzon ctenocephalus
(Roberts, 1982)
Gastromyzon scitulus
(Tan and Leh, 2006)

Synonyms: until recently, these two very similar species were known erroneously as *Gastromyzon punctulatus* by hobbyists around the world

Common Names: spotted hillstream loach, punktierter flossensauger (Germany)

Distribution: widespread

Occurrences: Kuamut headwaters, Kinabatangan Basin, Sabah, Malaysia
Baleh, Sarawak, Third Division; Baleh River, Sungei, Malaysia
Blomberg River, Kalimantan Timur, Indonesia
Sunghei Kuhas, Sadong River Basin, Sarawak, Borneo
Sunghei Ahi, Tebedu, Sarawak, Borneo

Habitat: fast-flowing water over boulders

Ideal Tank Parameters: pH 7.0 to 8.0; Temp 68° to 75°F (20° to 23.8°C)

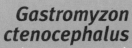
Gastromyzon ctenocephalus and G. scitulus

These two very similar species are easily confused. Hillstream enthusiasts have for years referred to them erroneously under the incorrect name of *Gastromyzon punctulatus*. The confusion likely originated due to original descriptions based on dead specimens. They are undeniably two of the most attractively colored and patterned hillstream

Which Fish is Which?

A special feature that is worthy of note is the red coloration of the nasal nares. The body coloration changes in shade, from yellowish to deep brown, depending on the surface the fish is resting on. This chameleon-like ability enhances the fish's already cryptic markings into an effective camouflage system. Although the fish keep their dorsal and caudal fins clamped shut most of the time, when moving or displaying to others they flash brilliant sky-blue with black markings. What were thought to be regional differences in the fin markings, body spot size, and distribution have now been clarified by the recent work of Dr. Tan Heok Hui, differentiating the two species. Dr. Tan has linked images of preserved specimens with those of live fish, greatly improving identification, particularly at the hobby level. The body spotting is variable within each species, but *G. scitulus* lacks the pale blue dorsal spotting of *G. ctenocephalus* and has a more intricate network of black on pale blue upon the caudal fin.

Gastromyzon stellatus. This attractive species has only recently been described. This specimen arrived in a shipment mixed with other Bornean *Gastromyzon*.

loaches, growing to about 1.8 inches (4.6 cm). Fortunately, they are exported somewhat regularly and are frequently available.

These two species, like others, are territorial and protective of their own space. They tend to stand their ground against other species unless the aggressor is substantially larger. A peculiarity of their behavior is that they seem to disappear from view within the aquarium at approximately 9 p.m. almost every night. It is as if they go to bed at that time.

In the wild, they eat small aquatic invertebrates living within algae (what the Germans call "aufwuchs") as they graze on rocks. In aquaria, flake foods, sinking pellets, algae wafers, frozen bloodworms, and brine shrimp will be eagerly accepted.

Sexual differences are not obvious, but generally females are plumper with a back profile that is more curved than that of a male. Neither species has been bred in an aquarium.

Sewellia lineolata

No single species has caused more of a stir among hillstream enthusiasts than the stunning *Sewellia lineolata*.

Since a picture of this species appeared on the front cover of a scientific publication, it has been at the top of most loach hobbyists' wish lists, but it has been available only on occasion since late 2004.

Arguably the most beautiful of all hillstream loaches, *S. lineolata* combines intricate bold black markings against a golden-yellow background. *S. lineolata* is distinguished from other members of its family by the presence of four parallel lines along the body sides, one of which is centered on the lateral line canal. The huge golden-copper eyes give the fish an alert look and indeed this fish has excellent visual acuity. Such large eyes are often associated with being nocturnal, but these fish are lively during times of bright light in nature and the aquarium. They are perhaps one of the most active examples of the sucker-bodied hillstream loaches. This only adds to their desirability in the home aquarium.

They do not seem to travel well and have little tolerance for crowding or oxygen shortage during transport, so care must be taken when choosing specimens in case they have suffered during their journey. Shippers are learning that these fish do suffer from overcrowding, which leads to prices higher than the regular prices associated with hillstream loaches.

Individuals are extremely defensive of their chosen area. When another of their species invades their territory they rush at it engaging in typical hillstream "topping" type behavior. These bouts of aggression can be quite prolonged and intense, yet seldom are any injuries sustained.

S. lineolata reaches about 2 inches (5 cm) and eats microscopic invertebrates combined with algae

Sewellia lineolata
(Valenciennes, 1849)

Synonyms: *Balitora lineolata* (Valenciennes in Cuvier & Valenciennes, 1849:99), *Sewellia lineolata* (Hora, 1932), *Sewellia lineolata* (Kottelat, 1944)

Common Names: reticulated hillstream loach, juovaimunuoliainen (Finland), sevelie pruhovaná (Czech Republic)

Distribution: China, Cambodia, and Vietnam

Occurrences: Conchinchine, Vietnam
Nam Nin River, Tra My District, Vietnam
Nuac Ta River, Tra My District, Vietnam
Quang Nan Province, Vietnam
Trac Khuc River, Nghai Bin Province, Vietnam
Tranh River, Tra My District, Vietnam

Habitat: fast-flowing rapids and riffles over boulders; small and large pools within small streams connected by riffles, sometimes with plants present; high-gradient streams with many waterfalls; upper extremities of riffle areas in larger rivers

Ideal Tank Parameters: pH 6.5 to 7.5; Temp 70° to 78°F (21° to 25°C)

rasped from rocks in nature. Compared to other hillstream loaches, they have very small mouths. This must be taken into consideration when offering aquarium foods. They will accept flakes, sinking pellets, algae wafers, frozen bloodworms, brine shrimp, and frozen *Mysis* shrimp. Some success has been had with offering slices of zucchini.

S. lineolata can be sexed quite easily in mature specimens. Adult males develop growths on the first few rays of the pectoral fins. These resemble a series of fences or louvers. Viewed from above, the leading edge of the pectoral fins is more squared off in relationship to the body. This gives the effect of males having square shoulders compared with the graduated curved line present in females. Like most other hillstreams, males tend to be noticeably dominant in behavior.

This species was first bred in aquaria by Emma Turner and Steve Rudd in Crowland, England in 2006. Spawning activity was not seen, but babies were discovered inside a canister filter. Others have witnessed pairs executing a kind of fluttering dance in which they rise together, belly to belly, and eggs and sperm are ejected. It appears that in nature the fish may scatter eggs in the current. No nest digging has been observed such as is seen with other hillstream species.

Homaloptera orthogoniata

Homaloptera orthogoniata is a beautiful and desirable fish that is unfortunately imported only on rare occasions. The fish do not seem to travel well and can be difficult to acclimatize to aquarium life. However, once they are used to aquarium conditions and the foods being offered, they can become long-lived and hardy. Somewhat larger than other hillstream species, they do not seem to attain maximum size in aquaria. Various occurrence

Homaloptera orthogoniata
(Vaillant, 1902)

Synonyms: none

Common Names: saddle-backed loach, gecko fish, orchid loach

Distribution: Indochina, Malay Peninsula, and Indonesia

Occurrences: Kapuas River Basin, Borneo, Indonesia
Sungai Pinoh River, Borneo, Indonesia
Sungai Tamang River, Borneo, Indonesia
Mekong River Basin, Laos
Muar River, Malaysia
Pahang River Basin, Malaysia
Tahan River, Malaysia
Sungai Tutoh River, Sarawak, Borneo, Malaysia
Sungai Ubong River, Sarawak, Borneo, Malaysia
Mekong River Basin, Thailand

Habitat: forest-lined streams; fast-flowing water over boulders

Ideal Tank Parameters: pH 6.5 to 7.5; Temp 70° to 78°F (21° to 25.5°C)

records in the wild report the fish were caught in "blackwater" conditions, a term usually used to describe soft acidic water stained by tannins.

They use their huge pectoral fins against the water flow, like racecar spoilers, to push themselves down upon a hard surface. They do not possess the sucker-like adaptations of other hillstream loaches.

In the aquarium, they will demonstrate their incredible sense of smell by reacting wildly when food is placed into the water. They will rush around, searching for food in a sort of frenzy, knocking other fishes out of the way as if oblivious of their presence. At a size of 5.1 inches (13 cm), they will obviously be able to knock smaller fishes aside. They are, however, not aggressive. They will spend a lot of the day hidden or just resting on a rock in the water's flow, saving their energy for high activity at feeding times. In nature, they probably eat tiny aquatic invertebrates that live within the algae they graze upon as well as small

While the basic layouts of the russet-red to brown markings on the pale pinkish body color are similar, apart from the stripe through the eye, no two *Homaloptera orthogoniata* appear exactly the same.

Loaches

189

Homaloptera orthogoniata.

worms. In aquaria, they will eat flake foods, sinking pellets, algae wafers, frozen bloodworms (which they eat with great abandon), and frozen brine shrimp.

H. orthogoniata has not been bred in aquaria. The fish seem to tolerate each other's company rather than directly challenge over territory like many other Balitoridae. Sexing is difficult, but some fish in aquaria regularly fatten up and then become suddenly slimmer. Most likely this would be females that release their eggs without any actual breeding occurring.

Homaloptera smithi

This 2.4 inch (6 cm) species is very similar in appearance and habits to *Homaloptera tweediei*. *H. smithi* seems to have more overlap of the pectoral and pelvic fins than *H. tweediei* and does not have the heavy markings of that species. Color is generally tan or brown. In addition, it has a much

Homaloptera smithi
(Hora, 1932)

Synonyms: *Homaloptera lineata*

Common Names: lizard fish, gecko fish, pa tit hin (Laotian)

Distribution: Mekong River Basin to Malay Peninsula

Occurrences: Mekong River Basin, Laos/Thailand/Cambodia/Vietnam
Sedili River, Malaysia
Terengan River, Malaysia
Tersat River, Malaysia
Dayame Chuang River, Myanmar
Sittang River, Myanmar
Chao Phraya River Basin, Thailand
Klong Pong Tadi Stream, Thailand
Mae Nam Tang River, Thailand
Me Ping River, Thailand
Menam Ping River, Thailand

Habitat: high-gradient, fast-flowing rapids over cobble runs and bedrock. Juveniles inhabit slower flowing areas with gravel and exposed tree roots

Ideal Tank Parameters: pH 7.0 to 8.0; Temp 68° to 75°F (20° to 23.8°C)

more stocky build than *H. tweediei* and is more like the sucker-belly types in appearance than other *Homaloptera*. There are no known sexual differences, and *H. smithi* has not bred in aquaria.

H. smithi is known to consume aquatic insect larvae, particularly odonatans. In aquaria, bloodworms are relished. The species will sometimes eat flakes, sinking pellets and brine shrimp.

Homaloptera smithi spends a lot of time grazing algae for tiny crustaceans.

Homaloptera tweediei

While this small species, reaching only 1.5 inches (4 cm), does not possess the full sucker-belly type adaptations of many other balitorids, it does have the remarkable ability to cling to surfaces. This ability is the reason it is called "gecko fish" in Thailand.

This fairly regularly imported species is variably colored, with a chameleon-like ability to change its color to suit its surroundings. It can vary from yellowish-brown to almost red. The markings consist of dorsal and lateral blotches with an often visible mid-lateral dark stripe. No visible sexual differences have been identified.

Homaloptera tweediei is extremely docile for a hillstream loach and can sometimes be quite retiring until settled into the aquarium. It has the endearing quality of having a bendable neck. The fish will turn its head as much as 45 degrees toward something of interest, and look around its habitat. This ability is extremely useful when creeping around the aquarium hunting for food. Coupled with the way the fish moves, the name "lizard fish" is more applicable to this species than its common use for other *Homaloptera* species. *H. tweediei* has been observed hunting fish fry, but normally it eats small aquatic invertebrates and zooplankton. In aquaria, the favorite food is frozen bloodworms. They will sometimes eat flakes.

Homaloptera tweediei
(Herre, 1940)

Synonyms: none

Common Names: lizard fish, gecko fish (Thailand)

Distribution: Mekong River Basin, Malay Peninsula, and Borneo

Occurrences: Kapuas River, Borneo, Indonesia
Sungai Engkonis, Borneo, Indonesia
Sungai Mandi Ketchil River, Borneo, Indonesia
Mawai District, Malaysia
Tok Dor River, Malaysia
Mekong River Basin, Laos/Thailand/Cambodia/Vietnam

Habitat: streams with moderate flow, having both live and dead vegetation. May move seasonally into flooded areas that have moderate flow

Ideal Tank Parameters: pH 7.0 to 8.0; Temp 68° to 75°F (20° to 23.8°C)

Homaloptera tweediei.

Homaloptera zollingeri
grows to 3.9 inches (10 cm)
and has no known sexual differences.

Homaloptera zollingeri
(Bleeker, 1853)

Synonyms: *Homaloptera javanica*, *Homaloptera nigra*

Common Names: lizard fish, suluser (Malay)

Distribution: Mekong River Basin to Malay Peninsula and Indonesia

Occurrences: Kapuas River, Borneo, Indonesia
Sungai Pinoh River, Borneo, Indonesia
Jelai River, Malaysia
Tandjong River, Malaysia
Mekong River Basin, Laos/Thailand/Cambodia/Vietnam
Bangpakong River, Thailand
Chao Phraya River Basin, Thailand
Meping River, Thailand

Habitat: high-gradient, fast-flowing streams over rocky substrate

Ideal Tank Parameters: pH 7.0 to 8.0; Temp 68° to 75°F (20° to 23.8°C)

Homaloptera zollingeri

This reclusive species is readily distinguishable from other *Homaloptera* species by the coloration of the caudal fin. The upper lobe is almost completely clear, while the lower lobe is darkly colored, appearing almost solid. Generally, *H. zollingeri* is also considerably darker in coloration than others of this genus. That feature and its somewhat larger eyes and retiring nature lead to the conclusion that it is largely nocturnal in its home waters. Aquatic insect larvae and other invertebrates are eaten in its native habitat. In aquaria, the species eats bloodworms, flakes, sinking pellets, and brine shrimp.

Liniparhomaloptera disparis disparis

This fish is seldom specifically imported, most often arriving as a contaminant in shipments of white-cheeked gobies (*Rhinogobius duospilus*), with which they share the same home streams. *Liniparhomaloptera disparis disparis* has, in the past, been described incorrectly in literature as *Homaloptera*

> The name **Homaloptera zollingeri** *has been wrongly associated with another species in aquarium literature in the past,* namely **Liniparhomaloptera disparis disparis.** *The latter is a far more lively fish during daylight hours.*

zollingeri and *Pseudogastromyzon myersi.*

This is one of the few species of hillstream loach to have been bred in captivity. The plump female fans a depression in the gravel with rapid swishes of the tail. She may dig several of these pits. Occasionally a male, or males, may assist in this digging. Sometimes she will dig herself into the gravel up to her dorsal fin. She will fine-tune the layout of the nest by pushing certain gravel particles or stones around with her nose. Nest sites are usually near the base of something solid such as a rock.

Eventually the fish will choose a site. The male sometimes assumes a position above the female with his snout touching the back of her head. He may then dart down beside her and quiver. The eggs will be laid and fertilized, and then the male will lose interest and leave the female to the task of covering the eggs. She will take great pains to make sure the surface of the nest matches the surrounding contours. The breeding process leaves her flushed and exhausted. After breeding, the female *L. disparis disparis* turns a light pink due to increased circulation. Her respiration level goes up significantly after all her nest digging, egg laying, and back filling of the nest. After spawning, the female retreats to a secluded spot to rest.

Once spawning activity starts, it may be repeated every two weeks. In about a week, fry may be seen between the particles of gravel if the nest is close to the aquarium glass. They will stay hidden for approximately two more weeks, emerging at approximately 0.4 inches (8 mm) in length. At this time, they have wide dark gray bands on the body, which provide excellent camouflage. They will

Liniparhomaloptera disparis disparis
(Lin, 1934)

Synonyms: *Homaloptera disparis, Liniparhomaloptera disparis, Linipaxhomaloptera disparis, Parhomaloptera disparis*

Common Names: broken-banded hillstream loach, lizard fish, plattschmerlen (German)

Distribution: southern China, northern Vietnam

Occurrences: Creeks above Pok Fulam Reservoir, Hong Kong, China Rivers surrounding Luofu Shan Mountain, China Rivers surrounding White Cloud Mountain, China Lam Tsuen River, China

Habitat: fast-flowing water over boulders

Ideal Tank Parameters: pH 7.0 to 8.0; Temp 68° to 75°F (20° to 23.8°C)

graze over all surfaces in the tank. Over the next two weeks, the adult body pattern will develop, taking several more weeks before its final pattern is reached. The young grow slowly, taking

Liniparhomaloptera disparis disparis lack the overlapping fins of some hillstream loaches, but are still able to withstand a strong current by directing water flow over their pectoral fins.

approximately five months to reach just over 1 inch (3 cm) in length. They attain sexual maturity at around six months and may begin breeding at this time. Maximum size is around 1.9 inches (5 cm).

L. disparis disparis is constantly active, grazing the rocks and plants for food. Individuals are hardy and eat most foods, but a high content of vegetable matter such as blanched kale or spinach leaves is desirable.

Pseudogastromyzon cheni

This is an active and hardy species, always on the go searching for food. Because of this, individuals make lively inhabitants for the specialized home aquarium. Despite being basically shades of brown, each individual fish will have unique markings. Like most of the dorso-ventrally compressed hillstream species, much of the time the dorsal fin is laid flat, but when making fast moves, or during territorial disputes with others, the beautiful dorsal fin is held open to display its red edge and yellow base marked with black dots. The eyes of this species are also quite distinctive, with the lower half being reflective silver.

This is one of the few hillstream species to have been bred in aquaria. Females are generally plumper, with a back profile that is more curved than that of a male. Both sexes have nasal tubercules, but in sexually active males these tubercles are more pronounced. During breeding times, the male's light and dark markings generally have more contrast than the female's.

Territorial protection by males is reduced when in breeding condition. At this time he will allow a chosen female into his area.

Courtship consists of the male frantically circling the female, fluttering his fins, with all his colors intensified. If she is

Pseudogastromyzon cheni
(Liang, 1942)

Synonyms: none

Common Names: Chinese hillstream loach, chinesischer flossensauger (Germany)

Distribution: widespread in Chinese highland streams

Occurrences: no records

Habitat: fast-flowing water over boulders

Ideal Tank Parameters: pH 7.0 to 8.0; Temp 68° to 75°F (20° to 23.8°C)

suitably impressed with his performance, she will follow him around the tank. The male normally digs several possible nest sites by sliding backwards off a rock and digging a spawning pit half under the rock with rapid swishes of his tail. Eventually the female will choose a pit that she finds attractive and the pair takes turns to enter, the male fertilizing the eggs laid by the female.

The pit is then covered by gravel to disguise its contents from predators and protect the eggs from the water current. For the first few days after hatching, the fry stay in the gravel, eventually finding their way to the top. At this time they are approximately 0.15 inch (4 mm) long and an almost

In *Pseudogastromyzon cheni*, the male's (left) nasal tubercules are more pronounced and the belly is more colorful.

uniform dark gray-brown in color. In a well-established tank, they will find plenty of food and soon grow to a size large enough that they can eat crumbled flake food and brine shrimp nauplii. Predation by the parents or others of the same species does not happen.

The babies soon resemble tiny replicas of their parents as their striped pattern develops. They will be seen actively grazing on the rockwork like a horde of little bugs. At this point, their growth tends to slow, and it takes as much as a year before they approach the adult size of 1.9 inches (5 cm) in the aquarium, even with regular feeding. In the wild they consume small aquatic invertebrates as they graze on algae growing on rocks. In aquaria, they eat flake foods, sinking pellets, algae wafers, frozen bloodworms, and brine shrimp. Blanched spinach and kale leaves are also well received in the aquarium.

> *Breeding of* P. cheni *has been accomplished by several aquarists. The one common factor in all successful breeding has been an abundance of water movement and aeration.*

Pseudogastromyzon sp.

Chapter 10

The Family Nemacheilidae

The fishes of the family Nemacheilidae, commonly referred to as the brook loaches, differ from the sucker-bodied hillstream loaches primarily in body shape and size of barbels as well as overall behavior and adaptation to currents. Members of this group share the same cool, well-oxygenated sand- and gravel-bottomed streams in temperate, tropical, and subtropical regions as the sucker-type balitorid species, but their range extends throughout Europe and into North Africa.

The Nemacheilidae, while not as physically adapted as their algae-grazing cousins, generally live in streams with strong flows. There are over 450 species in this group, all of which share the same basic characteristics. Their streamlined cylindrical bodies with enlarged pectoral fins allow the fish to move about or stabilize themselves in the moderate- to high-gradient streams with rock, sand, and pebble substrates in which they reside.

Barbel length, head and tail shape, and markings vary from species to species and can aid in identification of otherwise similar species. For instance, members of the genus *Nemacheilus* tend to have smaller heads, longer barbels, and more deeply forked tails than their *Schistura* cousins. Many *Schistura* show some sexual dimorphism. Males are notable for appearing to have inflated cheeks.

Acanthocobitis botia. The fishes of the family Nemacheilidae have much larger barbels than other loaches, giving them a somewhat catfish-like appearance. These barbels are equipped with sensory cells that aid in food location and probably in navigation through close quarters. Nemacheilidae species grub around and dig in the substrate to find food.

Food

Feeding is usually not a problem with members of the family Nemacheilidae. The mere introduction of food into the tank is enough to send many species into a feeding frenzy. This behavior can sometimes cause problems when several species are housed together. Placing food in various locations in the aquarium can often alleviate this competition. As with most other loaches, bloodworms are a favorite, but brine shrimp, pellets, and flakes are also accepted. Variety in their diet is important in maintaining good health.

Behavior and Tankmates

The boisterous and somewhat territorial behavior of the fishes in this group, particularly the larger species, may stress other fishes in the aquarium. They may also out-compete more timid species for food. Numerous hiding places will help alleviate territorial disputes (see Chapter 2). Although Nemacheilidae species live in habitats similar to those of the more highly specialized Balitoridae, their oxygen requirements are not so stringent, and they may be kept in tanks with more conventional setups as long as there is good filtration and aeration.

Reli River at 5,000 feet (1,500 m), near Kalimpong, West Bengal. Home to *Aborichthys*, *Acanthocobitis*, and *Schistura* spp.

There are important considerations when deciding which fishes to house with fishes of this group. Barbs, rasboras, danios, and other active stream fishes make good tankmates because they too are active feeders. *Botia* species and some of the larger, less shy hillstreams such as *Pseudogastromyzon* and *Protomyzon* species are also compatible. Most nemacheilid seem to enjoy being kept with others of the same or similar species if adequate territory is provided for each fish. Occasionally an overly territorial fish can become a problem. Having several fast-moving tankmates will reduce the chances of that loach's picking on one fish in particular.

Identification Problems

Several species of Nemacheilidae, primarily *Schistura* and *Nemacheilus*, are regularly available in the aquarium hobby, and the number of new species being imported is increasing. Positive identification, however, can be difficult because of close similarities between species. Common names such as sand loach, zebra loach, mountain loach, and red-tailed loach, which can be applied to numerous species, further complicate identification. As with the sucker-type hillstream loaches, shipments of these fishes can often contain numerous similar species. This makes positive identification an interesting and difficult proposition.

Aborichthys elongatus

Aborichthys elongatus is shaped like an elongated *Schistura*, hence the name. It reaches around 2.1 inches (5.4 cm). This is a peaceful but lively species, best suited to a river tank environment. In nature it inhabits fast-flowing streams at high altitudes; it needs current and cooler temperatures to feel at home. Individuals naturally hide under large boulders and stones and will appreciate plenty of hiding places within the aquarium. However, they are not a reclusive species and are constantly searching for food. They will dig into the substrate, often removing pieces of gravel in their mouths in order to access something that they have detected. They have excellent visual acuity and are well aware of their surroundings, reacting instantly when food is placed into the aquarium. They will swim rapidly to the surface to feed on floating flake food and when sitting on the substrate they quickly snap up any particles that drift past them. They will accept most regular aquarium foods, particularly relishing bloodworms and brine shrimp. Food size should be kept proportionately small, as these fishes are not big and have reasonably small mouths.

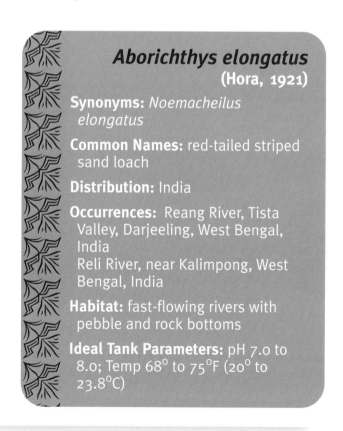

Aborichthys elongatus
(Hora, 1921)

Synonyms: *Noemacheilus elongatus*

Common Names: red-tailed striped sand loach

Distribution: India

Occurrences: Reang River, Tista Valley, Darjeeling, West Bengal, India
Reli River, near Kalimpong, West Bengal, India

Habitat: fast-flowing rivers with pebble and rock bottoms

Ideal Tank Parameters: pH 7.0 to 8.0; Temp 68° to 75°F (20° to 23.8°C)

A handsome adult specimen of *Aborichthys elongatus*.

Markings and coloration are extremely variable. Generally the base color is pale green-gray forward of the dorsal and more silvery-white behind it. Some fish have virtually no stripes forward of the dorsal, or may have a mottled pattern. There are greenish-gray stripes on the rear portion of the body in all individuals. Some may be completely striped with narrow banding, while others have quite wide bands. Consistent with all members of this species is a prominent eye spot at the upper edge of the caudal peduncle where it meets the caudal fin. The caudal fin is marked with variable numbers of curved bars and is generally reddish in coloration. Though there is much variability in the intensity of this color, basically the tail is light and dark red.

It is not known whether the differences in markings or color indicate sexual dimorphism.

Acanthocobitis botia

Acanthocobitis botia is a peaceful and very attractive loach that grows to a length of 4.25 inches (11 cm). Its silvery-gray body is marked by ten or more brown patches of various shapes and sizes that reach from the spine to midsection. A brown lateral line stretches from the gills to the caudal peduncle. On the upper part of the caudal peduncle is a prominent "eye spot" that is used to deceive predators. The belly is pale gray to white. The fins are spotted in loose rows of dark dots

Acanthocobitis botia
(Hamilton, 1822)

Synonyms: *Cobitis botia, Nemacheilus botia, Botia nebulosa, Botia mackenziei*

Common Names: zipper loach, mottled loach, eyespot loach, sand loach, bilturi (Bengali), chikli (Marathi), chitai (Hindi), gadera (Hindi), augenfleck Ceylon schmerle (German), modderkruiper (Dutch), bocja (Polish)

Distribution: Pakistan, India, Sri Lanka, Nepal, Bhutan, Bangladesh, Myanmar, Thailand, and China

Occurrences: Indus River Basin, Pakistan
Ganges River Basin, India
Brahmaputra River, India
Sarbhang Khola, Bhutan
Chindwinn River Basin, Myanmar
Irrawaddy River Basin, Myanmar
Salween River Basin, Myanmar
Sitoung River Basin, Myanmar
Chauhar River, Nepal
Bahuni River, Nepal
Gobraiya River, Nepal
Kali Gandaki River, Nepal
Koshi River, Nepal
Sunkoski River, Nepal
Tinau River, Nepal
Trisuli River, Nepal
Indus River, Pakistan
Leh River, Pakistan
Mae Khlong River Basin, Thailand
Yunnan Province, China

Habitat: clear, swift-flowing tropical streams and rivers with varying substrates of pebbles, gravel, and sand

Ideal Tank Parameters: pH 6.8 to 7.2; Temp 75.2° to 78.8°F (24° to 26°C)

along the fin rays. The caudal fin is more strongly marked, with four or five lines forming parallel V-shapes pointing toward the rear of the fish. The three pairs of barbels are relatively long and sensitive, giving the fish a keen sense of smell.

This species sifts sand and gravel through its gill slits, so it should be kept with a fine substrate. It consumes flake and dry pellet foods and relishes live or frozen bloodworms and daphnia. It will sometimes graze on algae.

Acanthocobitis rubidipinnis

A close relative of the zipper loach (*Acanthocobitis botia*), the cherry fin loach is slightly longer from head to tail at about 5 inches (13 cm). The dorsal fin is longer and more sail-like, with 14 to 15 dorsal rays. The eye is also smaller, and the relative length between the head and dorsal fin is shorter. Red coloration is present over the mouth, barbels, dorsal and pectoral fins, and tail. Their reticulated gray and brown markings assist camouflage and add to the fish's beauty.

These fish are strong swimmers, but they move more slowly through the water than other nemacheilids such as the *Schistura* species. Posterior of the dorsal fin the body is elongated and eel-like, giving the fish a very graceful appearance as they move about the tank.

> *In May and June, the noticeably fatter **A. botia** females lay a brood of 100 to 150 eggs in a hidden spot where they are fertilized by the male and left to hatch unattended.*

Acanthocobitis botia.

A. *rubidipinnis* has three pairs of distinctly long and flexible barbels that it uses to detect particles of food in the fine gravel substrate. These large barbels provide the fish with a heightened sense of smell. It is also able to pick up and move small pebbles in its constant quest for food. The cherry fin loach will readily eat flake food, frozen invertebrates, sinking wafers, and vegetables like blanched peas. Live insects and particles of food suspended in the current are favored, whereas aquatic plants are largely ignored.

This is an active and fearless loach that is diurnal in habit and spends less time in hiding than other nemacheilid species. It is well suited to a river tank and can be kept peacefully with hillstream loaches of all kinds, which it generally ignores. Competition and territorial skirmishes can be vigorous between individuals, but no real damage is ever inflicted.

Acanthocobitis rubidipinnis
(Blyth, 1860)

Synonyms: *Cobitis rubidipinnis, Cobitis semizonata, Noemacheilus rubidipinnis, Nemacheilus rubidipinnis*

Common Names: cherry fin loach, murangi (Kannada)

Distribution: Myanmar

Occurrences: Mandalay Division, Myanmar
Sagaing Division, Myanmar
Salween River System, Myanmar
Krishna River, India

Habitat: clear streams in northern Myanmar, central India; rocky substrate

Ideal Tank Parameters: pH 6.8 to 7.8; Temp 73.4° to 77°F (23° to 25°C)

The cherry fin loach (*Acanthocobitis rubidipinnis*) makes an excellent addition to the river tank.

Mesonoemacheilus triangularis
(Day, 1865)

Synonyms: *Nemacheilus triangularis, Nemachilus triangularis, Noemacheilus triangularis tambaraparniensis, Noemacheilus triangularis triangularis* (all no longer valid)

Common Names: batik loach, zodiac loach, koitha (Malayalam)

Distribution: India

Occurrences: Attingal River, India
Deviyar River, India
Kallar River, India
Periyar River, India
Western Ghats and Kerala, and Kanyakumari District of Tamil Nadu, India

Habitat: streams with pebble bottoms

Ideal Tank Parameters: pH 7.0 to 8.0; Temp 73° to 80°F (22.7° to 26.6°C)

Mesonoemacheilus triangularis

The combination of rich bronze color and worm-like gold markings make the 2.3-inch (6-cm) *Mesonoemacheilus triangularis* one of the most strikingly attractive fishes in this group. In addition, this species' feisty and inquisitive attitude makes it an engaging fish to keep in aquaria. While it will tolerate others of its species provided each has its own territory, this species can also be kept alone. During any fighting between one another, individuals will often change color from a faded gray to nearly black. *M. triangularis* is generally peaceful

Mesonoemacheilus triangularis.

toward other fishes. This species prefers more tropical temperatures than most other nemacheilines and accepts most aquarium foods.

Nemacheilus masyai

This very lively and active fish with attractive markings is a fairly common import in the aquarium trade. At 5.3 inches (13.5 cm), the size and high activity level of this fish can sometimes distress less active tank mates. Otherwise, this fish is relatively peaceful, but it will defend its territory.

Nemacheilus masyai
(Smith, 1933)

Synonyms: *Noemacheilus masyae, Nemacheilus masyae*

Common Names: arrow loach, mountain loach, checkerboard sand loach

Distribution: Cambodia, Malay Peninsula, peninsular Thailand

Occurrences: Trengganu River, Malaysia
Brang River, Malaysia
Nerus River, Malaysia
Chao Phraya River Basin, Thailand
Maeklong River Basin, Thailand
Mae Nam Nan River, Thailand
Tapi River Basin, Thailand

Habitat: rivers and streams with moderate current and mud or sand bottom

Ideal Tank Parameters: pH 7.0 to 8.0; Temp 68° to 78°F (20° to 25.5°C)

Nemacheilus masyai.

Nemacheilus pallidus
(Kottelat, 1990)

Synonyms: *Nemacheilus masyae* (misidentification)

Common Name: mountain loach

Distribution: Indochina

Occurrences: Mekong River Basin, Laos/Cambodia/Thailand/Vietnam
Tonle Sap Lake, Cambodia
Chao Phraya River Basin, Thailand
Maeklong River Basin, Thailand

Habitat: found in slower-current shallow streams with sand and mud bottoms

Ideal Tank Parameters: pH 7.0 to 8.0; Temp 68° to 78°F (20° to 25.5°C)

Nemacheilus pallidus

This active species that bears a strong resemblance to *Nemacheilus masyai* and was formerly misidentified as such. *N. pallidus* can be distinguished by its thicker body and thinner markings along the dorsal region. In *N. masyai* the markings are thicker than the space between them, while in *N. pallidus* they are thinner. *N. pallidus* grows to 5.5 inches (14 cm).

Nemacheilus pallidus.

The *Schistura* Species

The genus *Schistura* is a large and diverse group of nemacheilid loaches, containing around 200 species. That number will change, as new species have been discovered in recent years. Some are widespread over Southeast Asia while others may be confined to a single drainage. While there are variations in size and color patterns in this genus, there are also many species that are so similar that proper identification requires counting of stripes, spines, dorsal and caudal rays, or checking for the occurrence of a suborbital flap. Species such as *S.*

mahnerti, *S. vinciguerre*, and *S. subfusca*, to name a few, all have striped body patterns and red tails and can be very hard to identify properly. Accurate identification can be particularly difficult for the hobbyist when shipments of mixed species appear in local fish stores. Regardless of species, all *Schistura* are found in stream and river habitats. Their requirements of clean, flowing, well-oxygenated water can best be met by housing them in river or river pool tanks. For the purposes of this book, several commonly imported species are described in the following pages.

Schistura mahnerti.

Large numbers of *Schistura* species living in one area indicate very clean water. This photo shows numerous *Schistura* in the Dongwe River, western Thailand.

Schistura balteata

This attractive species is distinguished from other species by its unique markings and coloration. Two to three vertical bars extend below the dorsal fin. These form the transition point for the unusual bicolor body. The body is grayish in front of the stripes and yellow-orange to shades of pink behind the striping. *Schistura balteata* is similar in size and body shape to *S. scaturigina* at around 3.1 inches (8 cm). A generally shy species, it spends much of the day in hiding.

Schistura balteata
(Rendahl, 1948)

Synonyms: *Nemacheilus balteatus* (no longer valid)

Common Name: bicolor loach, sumo loach, sumu schmerle (Germany)

Distribution: Myanmar, Thailand, Malay Peninsula

Occurrences: Drainage of Khao Laem Reservoir, Myanmar
Tenasserim River Basin, Myanmar

Habitat: swift streams over rock and gravel bottoms

Ideal Tank Parameters: pH 7.0 to 8.0; Temp 68° to 78°F (20° to 25.5°C)

Schistura balteata.

Schistura beavani requires a soft substrate for burrowing.

Schistura beavani
(Gunther, 1868)

Synonyms: *Nemacheilus beavani, Noemacheilus beavani, Nemachilus beavani* (all no longer valid)

Common Names: banded loach, ring loach, creek loach, gadaula (Nepali)

Distribution: India and Nepal; reported from Bangladesh

Occurrences: Tista River, India/Bangladesh
Chitawan Valley, Nepal
Gaduala River, Nepal
Kanasha River, Nepal
Rapti River, Nepal

Habitat: pebble-bottom streams in highland areas; prefers pools and riffles

Ideal Tank Parameters: pH 7.0 to 8.0; Temp 68° to 78°F (20° to 25.5°C)

Schistura beavani

Schistura beavani reaches 2.4 inches (6 cm) and is fairly common in the aquarium trade. Large-eyed, attractively striped, and peaceful, it makes a nice addition to a small aquarium. *S. beavani* often digs into the substrate and may seek refuge there when frightened. Individuals have been observed in Nepal spawning in April and May.

Schistura corica
(Hamilton-Buchanan 1822)

Synonyms: formerly *Nemacheilus corica*

Common Names: polka dot loach, koirka (Bengali)

Distribution: India, Pakistan, Nepal, Bangladesh; also reported from Afghanistan
Salane River, India
Sarda River, India
Chitiwan Valley, Nepal
Kanasha River, Nepal
Koka River, Nepal
Indus River, Pakistan

Habitat: hill streams with sand bottoms

Ideal Tank Parameters: pH 7.0 to 8.0; Temp 68° to 78°F (20° to 25.5°C)

Schistura corica

Schistura corica is one of the most common of the small nemacheilids to be imported for the aquarium trade. Similar in length to *S. beavani* at 2.4 inches (6 cm), it is a bit more robust and boisterous. The spotted pattern varies greatly with each individual fish. The spots themselves grow larger and closer together as the fish matures. Another burrowing species, it requires a smooth substrate such as fine gravel or sand. *S. corica* eats most foods avidly in aquaria.

Schistura corica is commonly imported in the aquarium trade and requires a soft substrate for burrowing.

Schistura finis
(Kottelat, 2000)

Synonyms: none

Common Names: none

Distribution: Indochina

Occurrences: Nam Mo River Basin, Laos/Vietnam

Habitat: fast-flowing clear water in small creeks

Ideal Tank Parameters: pH: 7.0 to 7.4; Temp 72° to 80°F (22° to 26.6°C)

Schistura finis

This recently discovered species is still relatively rare in the aquarium trade. *Schistura finis* is a brightly colored loach with a red caudal fin and overall navy blue to gray body color. Twelve to 15 vertical bands of gray/brown run the length of its 3.5-inch (9-cm) body. The head of *S. finis* is large with swollen cheeks and a blunt snout. Three pairs of barbels are present.

S. finis is a territorial species that should be kept in small groups of three or more in larger river tanks with plenty of hiding spots. It is known to uproot plants and shred leaves during their constant quest for food. Meaty food such as bloodworms or tubifex worms should be offered regularly, although they will accept flake foods as well.

Schistura finis is an attractive and active loach for the river tank.

Schistura kohchangensis
(Smith, 1933)

Synonyms: *Nemacheilus deignani, Nemacheilus kohchangensis* (both no longer valid)

Common Names: ornate tiger sand loach

Distribution: Cambodia and Thailand

Occurrences: Chanlaburi, Chonburi, and Koh Chang Island, Thailand
Klong Salakpet, Thailand
Mekong River drainage, Cambodia/Thailand

Habitat: shallow high-gradient streams with gravel bottom in forested areas

Ideal Tank Parameters: pH 7.0 to 8.0; Temp 68° to 78°F (20° to 25.5°C)

Schistura kohchangensis

Another larger species, *Schistura kohchangensis* can be distinguished from other species by its long barbels. While young, this species is very active, often swimming back and forth at the front of the tank. But as it matures it tends to get more reclusive and sedentary. Mature males are distinguished by a suborbital flap. Occasionally, at night or at feeding time, it will have short bursts of activity similar to a juvenile fish. While not generally aggressive, its size of 2.95 inches (7.5 cm) and sometimes boisterous behavior can be unsettling to more timid tankmates.

Schistura kohchangensis.

Schistura kongphengi
(Kottelat, 1998)

Synonyms: none

Common names: none

Distribution: Mekong River Basin

Occurrences: Mekong River Basin, China/Laos/Thailand/Cambodia/Vietnam
Nam Theun River, Laos

Habitat: fast-flowing streams with gravel and boulder substrate

Ideal Tank Parameters: pH 6.8 to 7.8; Temp 68° to 78°F (20° to 25.5°C)

Schistura kongphengi

An uncommon *Schistura* species that grows to only 2.5 inches (6.5 cm). Seven to 13 vertical stripes and a lateral line are present, usually well contrasted to the silvery body color. Twelve soft rays are present in the dorsal fin. *S. kongphengi* requires well-aerated water.

Schistura mahnerti

Schistura mahnerti is another striped red-tailed species beginning to appear in the aquarium trade. This species, which grows to about 2.5 inches (6.5 cm), has up to 17 stripes along the length of the body. As in several other *Schistura* species, the stripes vary in form, according to their location on the body. Those toward the front of the body are

Schistura kongphengi.

Schistura mahnerti.

finer than those from the dorsal to the caudal fin. The caudal fin may vary greatly in the amount of red color present. Males have a suborbital flap that is absent in females. *S. mahnerti* can be an aggressive, territorial fish that may nip at the fins of slower-swimming species, so tankmates should be chosen carefully. Like other fishes of this group, *S. mahnerti* is a vigorous feeder and will accept meaty foods such as bloodworms and brine shrimp.

S. mahnerti is regularly misidentified as *S. vinciguerrae* or *S. subfusca*.

Schistura savona

Schistura savona is yet another small species occasionally found in the aquarium trade. Growing to only 1.1 inches (3 cm), it is typical of small *Schistura* species. *S. savona*, while active, is generally non-aggressive. Some minor territorial skirmishes between same or similar species may occur.

Schistura savona
(Hamilton, 1822)

Synonyms: *Nemacheilus savona* (no longer valid)

Common Names: half banded loach, savon khorka (Bengali)

Distribution: India, Bangladesh, and Nepal

Occurrences: Tista River Basin, India/Bangladesh
Kali River, India
Karnali River, India
Chitiwan Valley, Nepal
Naraini River, Nepal
Rapti River Basin, Nepal
Karnali and Kali drainages, Uttar Pradesh, India

Habitat: rapid-flowing streams with gravel bottoms

Ideal Tank Parameters: pH 7.0 to 8.0; Temp 68° to 78°F (20° to 25.5°C)

Schistura savona.

Schistura scaturigina
(McClennan, 1839)

Synonyms: *Nemacheius scaturigina, Nemacheilus schebbeuri, Nemachilus shebbearei, Noemacheilus scaturigina, Noemacheilus shebbearei, Nemacheilus zonatus, Nemachilus zonatus, Noemacheilus zonatus, Schistura zonata*

Common Names: victory loach, dari (Bengali)

Distribution: Bangladesh, Bhutan, India, and Nepal

Occurrences: Tributaries to the Tista and Jamuna Rivers, Bhutan/India/Bangladesh Chitiwan valley and tributaries of Rapi River, Nepal

Habitat: streams with gravel bottoms

Ideal Tank Parameters: pH 7.0 to 8.0; Temp 68° to 78°F (20° to 25.5°C)

Schistura scaturigina

Schistura scaturigina is one of the larger nemacheilids imported for the aquarium trade at 3.1 inches (8 cm). This is an attractive species with yellow base color and dark stripes. Most specimens have a "V"-shaped stripe pattern on at least one side of the body directly under the dorsal fin. The presence of this "V" led to the victory loach name for this species. Though large and somewhat boisterous, particularly at feeding time, *S. scaturigina* is less aggressive than many larger *Schistura* species. It spends much of the day in caves or other darker sheltered areas of the aquarium and will eat most foods.

Schistura vinciguerrae photographed in the Kasa River. The Kasa originates in Thailand and flows west through Myanmar, into the Bay of Bengal as part of the Salween River drainage.

Schistura vinciguerrae
(Hora, 1935)

Synonyms: *Nemacheilus putaoensis, Nemacheilus vinciguerrae, Nemachilus vinciguerrae, Noemacheilus vinciguerrae* (all no longer valid)

Distribution: China, India, Myanmar and Thailand.

Occurrences: Man Qiao He Stream, China
Irrawaddy River Basin, Myanmar/China
Putao River, Myanmar
Salween River Basin, Myanmar
North Pang Meton, Doi Nanka, Thailand

Habitat: Small streams with pebble bottoms and channels with very swift currents and smooth bottoms.

Ideal Tank Parameters: pH 7.0 to 8.0; Temp 68° to 78°F (20° to 25.5°C)

Schistura vinciguerrae

The 3.1-inch (8-cm) *Schistura vinciguerrae* is one of several large striped red-tailed *Schistura* species found in the aquarium trade. *S. vinciguerrae* can be identified by bars that are notably thinner in front of the dorsal fin than behind. Some specimens have red tails. The species is also known for its aggressive tendencies. *S. vinciguerrae* individuals are voracious feeders and should only be kept with suitably tough tank mates. Larger species of barbs and danios would be suitable companions.

An example of the many attractive but unidentified *Schistura* species that may arrive mixed in with named specimens. Without collection data, proper identification becomes extremely challenging.

Loaches

Afterword

In the relatively short time it took for this book to develop out of a humble manuscript, a lot has changed in the world of loaches. Had we started to write the book now, the featured species might be even more diverse. The general increase in demand for unusual species has led to new discoveries and exports of those fishes to hobbyists worldwide. We will cover a few of the most recently available species with some brief information.

Knowledge of the many Chinese loaches has increased in the last few years with exportation of a few species, but many desirable species are known in the West only from photographs. The fact that they may be kept successfully in unheated aquariums is a bonus, but it has led to legislation in Great Britain banning the import of certain species. This is because they may theoretically survive British temperatures if released into the wild by unscrupulous hobbyists, disrupting native species and the ecosystem.

One area that continues to change constantly is the nomenclature of loaches. There have been some detailed name changes, but the greatest area of change has been within the family Balitoridae (the hillstream loaches). When this book was first written, many species descriptions were known only from preserved specimens, and incorrect identification applied to living specimens became accepted internationally. True life colors may not appear in preserved fishes, so it is difficult to accurately identify living fishes from preserved specimens. Another occasional cause of incorrect identification was misleading text.

Because of the excellent work done by Dr. Tan Heok Hui and his team at the Raffles Museum of Biodiversity in Singapore, there are now multiple descriptions of known and new species which clarify these anomalies by directly linking

Some loach species are very fecund, so their natural breeding process can support a degree of collection during which the remaining population remains naturally sustainable, but this is not always the case. Studies are required to better understand the sustainability of wild populations of a given species, because many factors are involved. Environmentally damaging collection methods pose an even greater challenge for sustainability. Over-collection and destruction of the native habitat will adversely affect the population that is left or create unsuitable conditions for adequate repopulation of the species.

preserved material with photographs of living fishes. From a hobbyist's point of view, this makes correct identification far easier.

Color is an area where loaches as a family may thought to be lacking, but the pictures in this book show that despite background colors that may be earthy in nature, the photos are detailed with exquisite hues that make the fishes far more attractive than a casual observer may realize. This interest in attractive packaging may gradually diversify and develop into an interest in the behavioral quirks of certain species. Loaches are certainly high on quirky behavior and can be most entertaining. Bright colors and interesting habits are one reason for the popularity of the clown loach and have led to a rise in popularity of other loach species that feature bold markings and attractive coloration.

We added *Sewellia lineolata* into the Balitoridae descriptions after the original manuscript was finished because of the significant increase in popularity of the species that developed after the first imports arrived in the North America and Europe. The fish caused a sensation, raising the profile of hillstream loaches in general. The ornamental fish trade has been somewhat slow in recognizing the unique needs of these fishes, however, and we hope that this book will further the spread of knowledge regarding their specialized nature.

Another species of *Sewellia* has reached the West that does not properly match any described species. This new species is known as *Sewellia* sp. "spotted" due to the beautiful fine spotted pattern of adults. Emma Turner and Steve Rudd in Crowland, England, have bred both *Sewellia lineolata* and this species. The spotted species young go through completely amazing transformations in appearance as they develop and are extremely beautiful.

Schistura species are extremely variable, but apart from those many species that feature red fins they tend to lack bright colors. In 2006 and early 2007, two new undescribed species of *Schistura* entered the trade and have proven very popular among loach enthusiasts. The first is very similar to *Schistura balteata* and has been designated as *S.* cf. *balteata*. Examples with yellow or pink rear halves of the body co-exist in the same areas in the wilds of Thailand.

Sewellia sp. "spotted."

Schistura sp. "crimson."

Early in 2007 a shipment of *Schistura* species from Kerala, India arrived in Great Britain. Designated *Schistura* sp. "crimson," they feature intense red areas on the body. Over time in captivity, despite adequate and varied feeding, they lost some of their original color intensity. Could this be due to a lack of some specialized food item found in their habitat but unknown to the hobby? The supplier stated that these red *Schistura* specimens came from a protected forest area and are therefore unlikely to be captured again. This is yet another example of a fish that may come from one small area that may be severely impacted by over-collection.

Another *Schistura* species exported for the first time into Europe in the spring of 2007, *S. pridii* is a striking small white fish with bold black markings. Its export is a reason for concern, as it is found in a single small area, and over-exploitation would probably cause extinction in the wild. Several species of blind cave-dwelling *Schistura* and *Nemacheilus* have been described recently as well, but they may only occur in one small section of one river. These rare loaches are not for the aquarium trade, and their capture and export must be discouraged.

It is ironic that since this book began to take shape one species that had been available for many

Schistura pridii.

Yasuhikotakia sidthimunki.

years within the hobby has seen a huge turn-around in its availability. The beautiful and conveniently small *Yasuhikotakia sidthimunki* has been all but fished out in the wild. Our fish-keeping friends in Thailand were reporting that places where the fish were abundant during their childhood were now devoid of the species. This sad situation had led to spasmodic availability of the species within the hobby and correspondingly high prices. The ornamental fish trade has reacted to this lack of wild fish by finding the required triggers to allow the fish to breed in bulk in captivity, and now *Y. sidthimunki* is far more available than in 2003. In a few years we may be in the desirable situation of being able to re-introduce captive-bred fish back into their original habitats.

Five newly described species of kuhli loaches from India have appeared in scientific literature as recently as the spring of 2007. This delightful news came as something of a shock to many enthusiasts, who never imagined that this group of loaches would expand. But this clearly illustrates that we can expect our understanding of loaches to continue to change and expand in the years to come.

Loaches

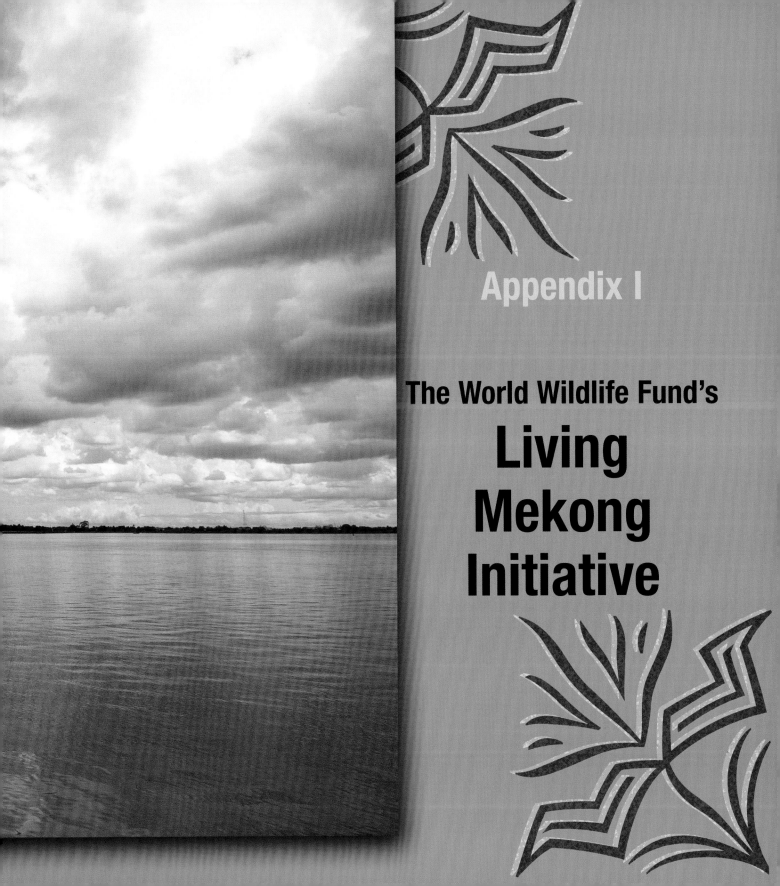

Appendix I

The World Wildlife Fund's
Living
Mekong
Initiative

The 2,982-mile- (4,800-km-) long Mekong running from the Tibetan Plateau to the South China Sea is one of the world's greatest rivers, home to over 1,200 species of fishes, including the endemic and endangered Mekong giant catfish. Each year 2 percent of the total fish consumption of the world comes from the Mekong Basin alone.

WWF Thailand, in collaboration with other WWF offices in the region, is working on the Living Mekong Initiative (LMI). WWF's vision for a "Living Mekong" is that "Healthy Freshwater Ecosystems are established and maintained that enhance and sustain livelihoods of local communities while ensuring the long-term

conservation of Mekong Basin biodiversity."

In line with this vision, WWF is actively advocating the adoption of and adherence to the World Commission on Dams (WCD) guidelines in relation to proposed development in the Mekong and its tributaries, such as the proposed NT2 dam in Laos, through our relationships with government agencies, the Mekong River Commission, and Multilateral Development Banks—the Asian Development Bank (ADB) and the World Bank (WB).

We are also applying similar criteria to the proposed rapids blasting for improved navigation in the Mekong, supporting the efforts of the "Rak Chiang Khong" group who are calling for a

professional EIA process and real public dialogue on this issue. Mekong conservation activities also include annual Dhamma pilgrimage boat journeys on the Mekong with Buddhist clergy from the Sekyitham group, and other awareness-raising initiatives. In the future, WWF will work with schools in Loei Province to develop the first "local curriculum" on the Mekong River, serving as a model for other provinces, and eventually for neighboring countries.

Destructive Fishing and Dams Threaten the Mighty River

The Mekong is one of the world's great rivers, sustaining millions with its rich fishery and fertile flood plains. Home to an estimated 1,200 species of fishes, the wealth of its biodiversity is comparable to that of the Amazon River. But the giant catfish, one of the largest freshwater fish in the world and endemic to the Mekong, appears to be on the brink of collapse while the river's population of Irrawaddy dolphins numbers less than 100. Destructive fishing practices, the construction of hydroelectric dams, and the improvement of navigation channels threaten the river's integrity. The Living Mekong Initiative is addressing these dangers and providing solutions to the pressing problems of population growth and unsustainable development.

Fertile Delta is Indochina's Rice Bowl

Fed by the melting snow of the Tibetan Himalayas and seasonal monsoon rains, the Mekong River runs through six countries from China in the north to the south to Myanmar, Laos, Thailand, Cambodia, and finally Vietnam before spilling into the South China Sea. Its catchment area covers 309,000 square miles (800,000 km²), encompassing an extraordinary range of vegetation and bio-

geographical features. Long considered Indochina's rice bowl, the river's vast delta is the most productive agricultural land in the region, responsible for half the rice grown in Vietnam and a source of food for nations around the world. Recent political struggles in the Indochina peninsula have protected the Mekong Basin from the dramatic changes in the landscape and the flood patterns that have decimated the natural biology of many of the world's rivers. In spite of the pressure from a growing population, the Mekong is still relatively intact, offering the region a golden opportunity to become a model for sustainable development by strengthening the economy and improving the living standards of its people without destroying the environment.

The river and the many tributaries that feed into it are home to over 60 million people comprising upwards of 95 distinct ethnic groups. The majority of the population is supported by the flood plain, which, because of the richness of the soil, regenerated regularly by the annual floods, has become the focus of development. However, the expanding network of dikes and roads and the increasing construction of hydroelectric dams are altering the natural process, disrupting the natural replenishment of agricultural soils and fish yields and contributing to the ever-increasing severity and frequency of the floods. Moreover, these dikes and dams are badly damaged during the floods, and the cost of constantly repairing and replacing them is a major drain on scarce funds earmarked for development.

WWF Considers the Benefits of Living with Floods

The Living Mekong Initiative, a joint program of WWF Indochina and WWF Thailand, is promoting the concept of "living with the floods." This involves moving non-submersible activities which sustain the greatest damage during floods off the flood plains and away from the destructive power of the river, while at the same time advocating infrastructure that can withstand the floods and is less obstructive and vulnerable. A comprehensive approach is also being urged so to ensure that these structures do not have a negative impact on downstream villages.

One of the initial steps being taken with this aim is to identify the human activities that benefit from the annual floods, and the different options for developing the flood plains. The results of this analysis will then be used to compare the benefits of living with the flood to the benefits and costs of large flood-protection infrastructure. The first analysis focuses on the flood plains of southern Laos and Cambodia. As part of its Mekong Initiative, WWF Indochina is also working with the French Development Agency (AFD, the initialization of the agency's name in French) to study the effect of the floods on three recently

constructed bridges on a portion of a road in the Mekong flood plain. The study will look at the stability of the bridges and the bridges' impact on how the shape of the river alters and on flood flows on a larger scale. The results of this study are expected to change the way roads are planned and bridges and culverts are designed so that they are better able to withstand the floodwaters and obstruct the natural flow less.

Construction of Dams Monitored

The release of the report of the World Commission on Dams (WCD) in 2000 is changing the way issues regarding dams are tackled in the Mekong Basin. Yet most stakeholders involved don't know about the report and need assistance just to follow the recommendations. The Living Mekong Initiative is participating in WWF's Global Campaign on Dams by monitoring the implementation of WCD recommendations for two local dam projects: Nam Theun 2 in Laos and Ta Trach in central Vietnam.

WWF Indochina's work on the Mekong River is greatly assisted by a unique partnership among the four countries of the lower basin—Cambodia, Laos, Thailand, and Vietnam—which in 1995 signed a cooperative agreement for the sustainable development of the Mekong River Basin. This

agreement formally established the present day Mekong River Commission to enable collaboration on regional river development issues. A memorandum of agreement signed between WWF Indochina and the Commission allows the Living Mekong Initiative to work with one unique and major partner: the Commission's secretariat.

The Commission is currently developing a social atlas of the Lower Mekong Basin, to which the Living Mekong Initiative is contributing information about the environment. WWF Indochina will also assist the Commission to assess of the biodiversity of the Lower Mekong.

China's Plans Pose a Major Obstacle

However, plans by China, which is not a member of the Commission, to build a series of dams on the mainstream of the Mekong and to dredge the upper part of the river to improve navigation constitute a major obstacle to the success of the Commission and threaten the livelihoods of fishers and farmers living along the southern stretches of the Mekong. WWF's Living Mekong Initiative aims to ensure more involvement of stakeholders in China who would benefit if there were no large infrastructure projects such as hydroelectric dams on the upper Mekong.

Alternatives to large hydroelectric dams were considered at a workshop organized recently by the WWF Indochina, IUCN, and the Commission. One of the priorities of the workshop, which was attend by high-level officials from the energy ministries of the Mekong River countries, was to determine more accurately how much energy will be required in the future. Recent studies in Thailand have shown that the demand for electricity expected in the future has been overestimated, thus making the calls for more dams unnecessary.

Future climatic conditions are also being addressed. The Mekong River Basin is one of three areas worldwide where WWF is integrating the activities of its Freshwater and Climate Change programs. WWF's Asia-Pacific's Climate Change Program, and the Living Mekong Initiative, are collaborating to enhance joint strategies. WWF Indochina will identify the areas in the Mekong Basin that are the most susceptible to the impact of climate change and enhance the ability of governments to address the problems of changing rain patterns and rising sea levels, which pose their own dangers to the river.

Visit wwfindochina.org for more information.

Current Taxonomic Table of the Family Botiidae

Taxonomic changes were made in the subfamily Botiinae by Dr. Maurice Kottelat, who described two new genera, *Yasuhikotakia* and *Chromobotia*, in 2004. Old names for the genera *Leptobotia*, *Parabotia*, *Sinibotia*, and *Syncrossus* were also reinstituted. In 2007, analysis from nuclear genetic data by Vendula Šlechtová, Jörg Bohlem, and Heok Hui Tan led to reclassification of Bottiinae as being separate from Cobitoidae. The family of Botiidae was created.

Current name contains currently valid species names.
Name contains all known names, valid and synonymous.
Author is the original author of published information on the species named.
Year contains the year of publication in which the "Name" was published for the first time.

Current name	Name	Author	Year
Botia almorhae	*Botia almorhae*	Shrestha	1978
Botia almorhae	*Botia grandis*	Gray	1832
Botia almorhae	*Botia lohachata*	Chaudhuri	1912
Botia almorhae	*Schistura maculata*	McClelland	1839
Botia birdi	*Botia birdi*	Chaudhuri	1909
Botia birdi	*Botia javedi*	Mirza & Syed	1995
Botia blythi	*Botia blythi*	Bleeker	1863
Botia dario	*Botia dario*	Day	1878
Botia dario	*Botia dario*	Talwar & Jhingran	1991
Botia dario	*Botia geto*	Talwar & Jhingran	1991
Botia dario	*Canthophrys zebra*	Swainson	1839
Botia dario	*Cobitis dario*	Hamilton	1822
Botia dario	*Cobitis geto*	Hamilton	1822
Botia dario	*Diacantha flavicauda*	Swainson	1839
Botia dario	*Diacantha zebra*	Swainson	1839
Botia dario	*Hymenphysa dario*	McClelland	1839
Botia histrionica	*Botia histrionica*	Blyth	1860
Botia kubotai	*Botia kubotai*	Kottelat	2004
Botia macrolineata	*Botia macrolineata*	Teugels, De Vos & Snoeks	1986
Botia pulchripinnis	*Botia pulchripinnis*	Paysan	1970
Botia rostrata	*Botia rostrata*	Günther	1868

Current name	Name	Author	Year
Botia striata	*Botia striata var. kolhapurensis*	Kalawar & Kelkar	1956
Botia striata	*Botia striata*	Narayan Rao	1920
Botia striata	*Botia striata*	Rao & Seshachar	1927
Botia variegata	*Botia variegata*	Günther	1889
Botia yunnanensis	*Botia yunnanensis*	Chen	1980
Chromobotia macracanthus	*Botia macracantha*	authors	
Chromobotia macracanthus	*Botia macracanthus*	Roberts	1989
Chromobotia macracanthus	*Chromobotia macracanthus*	Kottelat	2004
Chromobotia macracanthus	*Cobitis macracanthus*	Bleeker	1852
Leptobotia curta	*Botia curta*		
Leptobotia curta	*Capoeta curta*	Temminck & Schlegel	1846
Leptobotia curta	*Hymenophysa curta*	Okada	1961
Leptobotia curta	*Leptobotia curta*	Sawada in Masuda et al.	1984
Leptobotia elongata	*Botia citrauratea*	Nichols	1925
Leptobotia elongata	*Botia elongata*	Bleeker	1870
Leptobotia elongata	*Leptobotia elongata*	Bleeker	1870
Leptobotia elongata	*Leptobotia elongata*	Ding	1994
Leptobotia flavolineata	*Leptobotia flavolineata*	Wang	1981
Leptobotia guiliensis	*Leptobotia guiliensis*	Chen	1980
Leptobotia hengyangensis	*Leptobotia hengyangensis*	Huang & Zhang	1986
Leptobotia intermedia	*Leptobotia intermedia*	Mori	1929
Leptobotia kudoii	*Leptobotia kudoii*	Mori	1933
Leptobotia mantschurica	*Leptobotia hopeiensis*	Shaw & Tchang	1931
Leptobotia mantschurica	*Leptobotia mantschurica*	Berg	1907
Leptobotia microphthalma	*Leptobotia microphthalma*	Fu & Ye	1983
Leptobotia orientalis	*Leptobotia orientalis*	Xu, Fang & Wang in Wang	1984
Leptobotia pellegrini	*Leptobotia pellegrini*	Fang	1936

Current name	Name	Author	Year
Leptobotia posterodorsalis	*Leptobotia posterodorsalis*	Lan & Chen in Chen & Lan	1992
Leptobotia rubrilabris	*Botia pratti*	Günther	1892
Leptobotia rubrilabris	*Leptobotia rubrilabris*	Ding	1994
Leptobotia rubrilabris	*Parabotia rubrilabris*	Guichenot in Dabry de Thiersant	1872
Leptobotia taeniops	*Botia purpurea*	Nichols	1925
Leptobotia taeniops	*Leptobotia taeniops*	Ding	1994
Leptobotia taeniops	*Parabotia taeniops*	Sauvage (ex Guichenot)	1878
Leptobotia tchangi	*Leptobotia tchangi*	Fang	1936
Leptobotia tientainensis	*Botia compressicauda*	Nichols	1931
Leptobotia tientainensis	*Botia tientainensis*	Wu	1930
Leptobotia tientainensis	*Leptobotia hansuiensis*	Tang et al.	2001
Leptobotia tientainensis	*Leptobotia tientainensis hansuiensis*	Fang & Hsu	1980
Leptobotia tientainensis	*Leptobotia tientainensis*	Zhu	1995
Leptobotia zebra	*Botia zebra*	Wu	1939
Leptobotia zebra	*Leptobotia zebra*	Kottelat	2004
Parabotia banarescui	*Leptobotia banarescui*	Nalbant	1965
Parabotia banarescui	*Parabotia banarescui*	Kottelat	2004
Parabotia bimaculata	*Parabotia bimaculata*	Chen	1980
Parabotia fasciata	*Parabotia dubia*	Kottelat	2001
Parabotia fasciata	*Botia elongata*	Mai	1978
Parabotia fasciata	*Botia kwangsiensis*	Fang	1936
Parabotia fasciata	*Botia multifasciata*	Regan	1905
Parabotia fasciata	*Botia wui*	Chang	1944
Parabotia fasciata	*Botia xanthi*	Wang	1984
Parabotia fasciata	*Hymenophysa kwangsiensis*	Fang	1936
Parabotia fasciata	*Leptobotia fasciata*		
Parabotia fasciata	*Nemacheilus xanthi*	Günther	1888

Current name	Name	Author	Year
Parabotia fasciata	*Nemachilus xanthi*	Günther	1888
Parabotia fasciata	*Nemachilus xanthi*	Günther	1888
Parabotia fasciata	*Parabotia fasciata*	Dabry de Thiersant	1872
Parabotia fasciata	*Parabotia fasciata*	Ding	1994
Parabotia fasciata	*Parabotia fasciata*	Guichenot in Dabry de Thiersant	1872
Parabotia fasciata	*Parabotia fasciatus*	Guichenot in Dabry de Thiersant	1872
Parabotia lijangensis	*Parabotia lijangensis*	Chen	1980
Parabotia maculosa	*Botia maculosa*	Wu	1939
Parabotia maculosa	*Parabotia maculosa*	Kottelat	2004
Parabotia parva	*Parabotia parva*	Chen	1980
Sinibotia longiventralis	*Botia longiventralis*	Yang & Chen	1992
Sinibotia longiventralis	*Sinibotia longiventralis*	Yang & Chen	1992
Sinibotia pulchra	*Botia gigantea*	Mai	1978
Sinibotia pulchra	*Botia pulchra*	Wu	1939
Sinibotia pulchra	*Sinibotia pulchra*	Kottelat	2004
Sinibotia reevesae	*Botia reevesae*	Chang	1944
Sinibotia reevesae	*Sinibotia reevesae*	Kottelat	2004
Sinibotia robusta	*Botia dayi*	Hora	1932
Sinibotia robusta	*Botia hexafurca*	Mai	1978
Sinibotia robusta	*Botia robusta*	Wu	1939
Sinibotia robusta	*Sinibotia robusta*	Kottelat	2004
Sinibotia rubrilabris	*Botia fangi*	Tchang	1930
Sinibotia superciliaris	*Botia superciliaris*	Günther	1892
Sinibotia superciliaris	*Sinibotia superciliaris*	Kottelat	2004
Syncrossus beauforti	*Botia beauforti var. formosa*	Pellegrin & Fang	1940
Syncrossus beauforti	*Botia beauforti*	Smith	1931
Syncrossus beauforti	*Botia formosa*	Kottelat	2001

Current name	Name	Author	Year
Syncrossus beauforti	*Botia lucas-bahi*	Fowler	1937
Syncrossus beauforti	*Botia lucasbahi*	Fowler	1937
Syncrossus beauforti	*Syncrossus beauforti*	Kottelat	2004
Syncrossus berdmorei	*Botia berdmorei*	Talwar & Jhingran	1991
Syncrossus berdmorei	*Syncrossus berdmorei*	Blyth	1860
Syncrossus helodes	*Botia helodes*	Sauvage	1876
Syncrossus helodes	*Syncrossus helodes*	Kottelat	2004
Syncrossus hymenophysa	*Botia hymenophysa*	Kottelat	1984
Syncrossus hymenophysa	*Botia hymenophysa*	Roberts	1989
Syncrossus hymenophysa	*Cobitis hymenophysa*	Bleeker	1852
Syncrossus hymenophysa	*Hymenophysa macclellandi*	Bleeker	1858-59
Syncrossus hymenophysa	*Hymenophysa macclellandi*	Bleeker	1858-59
Syncrossus hymenophysa	*Hymenophysa macclellandi*	Bleeker	1859
Syncrossus hymenophysa	*Syncrossus hymenophysa*	Kottelat	2004
Syncrossus reversa	*Botia reversa*	Roberts	1989
Syncrossus reversa	*Syncrossus reversa*	Kottelat	2004
Yasuhikotakia caudipunctata	*Botia caudipunctata*	Taki & Doi	1995
Yasuhikotakia caudipunctata	*Yasuhikotakia caudipunctata*	Kottelat	2004
Yasuhikotakia eos	*Botia eos*	Taki	1972
Yasuhikotakia eos	*Yasuhikotakia eos*	Kottelat	2004
Yasuhikotakia lecontei	*Botia lecontei*	Fowler	1937
Yasuhikotakia lecontei	*Yasuhikotakia lecontei*	Kottelat	2004
Yasuhikotakia longidorsalis	*Botia longidorsalis*	Taki & Doi	1995
Yasuhikotakia longidorsalis	*Yasuhikotakia longidorsalis*	Kottelat	2004
Yasuhikotakia modesta	*Botia modesta*	Bleeker	1865
Yasuhikotakia modesta	*Botia rubripinnis*	Sauvage	1876
Yasuhikotakia modesta	*Yasuhikotakia modesta*	Kottelat	2004

Current name	Name	Author	Year
Yasuhikotakia morleti	*Botia horae*	Smith	1931
Yasuhikotakia morleti	*Botia morleti*	Tirant	1885
Yasuhikotakia morleti	*Yasuhikotakia morleti*	Kottelat	2004
Yasuhikotakia nigrolineata	*Botia nigrolineata*	Kottelat & Chu	1987
Yasuhikotakia nigrolineata	*Hymenophysa nigrolineata*	Kottelat & Chu	1987
Yasuhikotakia nigrolineata	*Yasuhikotakia nigrolineata*	Kottelat	2004
Yasuhikotakia sidthimunki	*Botia sidthimunki*	Klausewitz	1959
Yasuhikotakia sidthimunki	*Yasuhikotakia sidthimunki*	Kottelat	2004
Yasuhikotakia splendida	*Botia splendida*	Roberts	1995
Yasuhikotakia splendida	*Yasuhikotakia splendida*	Kottelat	2004

# Biographies

Mark Macdonald

Mark Macdonald fell in love with loaches as he first discovered the aquarium hobby and has focused his attention on accommodating their needs through tank design. Through the pursuit of better loach keeping, he managed to meet his co-authors and has struck up many long-lasting friendships. Along with loaches, Mark's interests include natural history, botany, ornithology, and conservation. He is the author and editor of a number of books of both fiction and nonfiction. He and his partner live in Delta, British Columbia with their famous cat, Nico.

Martin Thoene

Martin Thoene has kept fish since 1964. After a brief period working in the aquarium fish import trade, he decided to get a real job and relegate fish to purely a hobby. His interest in loaches began in 1998 and his innovation of the river tank manifold enabled hobbyists worldwide to keep hillstream loaches successfully. Martin lives in Toronto after emigrating from England in 2001. He lives in a penthouse apartment with too many fish tanks. His articles and photographs have been published in magazines and online articles have been translated into several languages.

Shari Sanford

A relative newcomer to loaches, Sharon Sanford was seduced into loachaholism by a domineering *Yasuhikotakia eos* in 2004. Proud mom of a US Marine, she lives in New Jersey with her husband, five of her seven children, a dog, seasonal snakes, and the occasional lost or injured wild creature along with an ever fluctuating number of fish tanks. Fascinated by chemistry and parasitology, she has contributed an article to Loaches Online, "Levamisole Hydrochloride – Its Application and Usage in Freshwater Aquariums," and continues research related to diseases and treatments of freshwater fish, especially loaches.

Barbara McEntee

The dimensions of a 55-gallon aquarium captured Barbara McEntee's visual aesthetic and 13 tanks of proliferating livebearers later, her fish breeding mini-business downsized to focus on *Synodontis petricola* catfish exclusively. For sheer enjoyment she also keeps a variety of loaches that are adored for their intelligence and curiosity. Influenced by years of meditation practice, respect for all sentient beings, and a life-long association with education, Barbara's primary aquatic interest has been in providing a healthful environment for her fish and sharing that experience and knowledge with others. Her current challenge is how to keep aquariums in her new off-the-grid location in rural Maine.

Robin Lynn

Robin Lynn is a journalist in New York whose career has included stints with various media companies including CBS News and *PC Magazine*. Crediting her mother Nelda for imparting a life-long love of animals, Robin was first exposed to the world of home aquaria as a child after winning a goldfish at a church fair. Years later she fell in love with loaches upon acquiring a trio of clowns as a natural solution to an outbreak of ramshorn snails. Her motto is, "Loaches are like potato chips, you can't ever have just one." Robin shares her home with nine different species of loach, her own personal coral reef, and a small pride of Siamese cats.

James Powers

Jim Powers lives in Bloomington, Indiana and has been in the hobby off and on since childhood when his patient parents allowed him to keep a large and varied menagerie of small creatures. For the last several years, he has been focusing on loaches. Jim has kept over 30 species of loaches including botiid, brook, and hillstream loaches and a few miscellaneous species. He has successfully bred some hillstream loach species and co-authored an article on the subject with Martin Thoene. Jim has also been a guest speaker at various aquarium club meetings and conventions, giving presentations on loaches.

Michael Ophir

Michael Ophir is a senior at Wheaton College in Norton, Massacheucetts majoring in biochemistry. He has been observing fish in his home aquariums since the age of five. He has published several articles on loaches in popular aquarium magazines and is particularly interested in botiid species. He would like to thank his parents Shalom and Ellen Ophir and brother Alex Kanevsky for their continued support throughout his studies and passion for the aquarium fish hobby.

Resources

Magazine

Tropical Fish Hobbyist
1 TFH Plaza
3rd & Union Avenues
Neptune City, NJ 07753
E-mail: info@tfh.com
www.tfhmagazine.com

Internet Resources

Aquaria Central
www.aquariacentral.com

Aquarium Hobbyist
www.aquariumhobbyist.com

FishBase
www.fishbase.org

Fish Geeks
www.fishgeeks.com

Loaches Online
www.loaches.com

Planet Catfish
www.planetcatfish.com

Tropical Resources
www.tropicalresources.net

Wet Web Media
www.wetwebmedia.com

A World of Fish
www.aworldoffish.com

Books

Hui, T. 2006. *The Borneo Suckers: Revision of the Torrent Loaches of Borneo.* Natural History Publications, Borneo.

Loiselle, P.V. c.1970s. *Catfish and Loaches: The Bottom Dwellers.* Tetra Press.

Loiselle, P.V. and D. Pool. 1993. *Hobbyist Guide to Catfish and Loaches.* Tetra Press.

Walker, B. 1974. *Sharks and Loaches.* TFH Publications, Inc., New Jersey, United States.

Index

Note: **Boldfaced** numbers indicate illustrations; an italic *t* indicates a table.

ich (*Ichthyopthirius multifilis*) in, 76, 77, 86, 87–90, **89**
internal parasites and, 86–87
medications in, 86
observation to spot, 86
Pangio spp. (Kuhli loach) and, 150–151
prevention of disease and, 94–95
salt treatment in, 89
septicemia and, 90
signs of good health in, 77
sterilization of filters and, 83
stress and, 79, 95
toxicity of medications and, 90
transporting fish and, 79–80
velvet (*Piscinoodinium*) in, 76, 86, 93–94, **93**
worms as internal parasites, 86
heat treatment for disease, 89–90
heaters, 30
Hemimyzon spp., 22
hiding spots
for *Botia histrionica* (Burmese loach), 116
for *Botia kubotai* (Angelicus loach), 118
for *Chromobotia macracanthus* (Clown loach), 102
for *Yasuhikotakia morleti* (Skunk loach), 135
for *Yasuhikotakia nigrolineata* (Black-lined loach), 136
Hieroglyphic loach. *See Leptobotia guilinensis*
hillstream loaches, health issues in, 77, 94
Homaloptera spp., 22, 182
   H. bilineata, 189
   H. cf. oglivie, 189
   H. confuzona, 189
   H. orthogoniata (Saddle-backed loach), 188–190, **189**
   H. smithi (Lizard fish), 190, **191**
   H. tweedie (Lizard fish), 192, **192**
   H. zollingeri (Lizard fish), 193, **193**, 194
homemade loach food recipe, 71
Honey gourami. *See Trichogaster chuna*
Hong Kong pleco. *See Beaufortia kweichowensis*
Hora's loach. *See Yasuhikotakia morleti*
Horseface loach. *See Acantopsis choirorhynchus*
Horsehead loach. *See Acantopsis choirohynchus*
hospital tanks, 82–83. *See also* quarantine
Hyemophysa macclellandi. *See Syncrossus hymenophysa*
hymenophysa complex, 99, 122. *See also Syncrossus* spp.
Hymenophysa curta. *See Leptobotia curta*
Hymenophysa kwangsiensis. *See Parabotia fasciata*
Hymenophysa nigrolineata. *See Yasuhikotakia nigrolineata*
Hymenphysa dario. *See Botia dario*
Hypsibarbus wetmirei (Lemon-finned barbs), 56

I
ich (*Ichthyopthirius multifilis*), 76, 77, 86, 87–90, **89**
India, 6, 13
Indochina, 13, 18
Indonesia, 13
induced drag, 177
internal parasites, 86–87
International Union for Conservation of Nature and Natural Resources (IUCN),

138, 235
Ireland, 18
Irian Jaya, 18
Irrawaddy river, 25
Israel, 18

J
Jabo. *See Botia almorhae*
Java loach. *See Pangio oblongata*
Java fern. *See Microsorum pteropus*
Jordan, 18
Juovaimunuoliainen. *See Sewellia lineolata*

K
Kanevsky, Alex, 245
Kasa River, **76**
Keeogai. *See Yasuhikotakia modesta*
Koirka. *See Schistura corica*
Koitha. *See Mesonoemacheilus triangularis*
Krawhorn. *See Yasuhikotakia eos; Y. modesta*
Kuhli loach. *See Pangio kuhlii*

L
Ladderback loach. *See Yasuhikotakia sidthimunki*
Langli. *See Syncrossus hymenophysa*
Laos, 20, 21, 22, 230, 231, 233
Lasawuma stream, as source of Mekong, 20
Lebanon, 18
Leiterschmerle. *See Botia dario*
Lemna spp., 59
Lemon-finned barbs. *See Hypsibarbus wetmirei*
Leopard eel. *See Pangio kuhlii*
Lepidocephalichthys spp., 22
L. guntea (Peppered loach), 167–168, **168**
Leptobotia spp., 101, 143–145
   L. banarescui. See Parabotia banarescui
   L. curta, 239t
   L. elongata, 239t
   L. fasciata. See Parabotia fasciata
   L. flavolineata, 239t
   L. guilinensis (Chinese golden tiger loach), **73**, 143–145, **144**, 239t
   L. hansulensis. See L. tientainensis
   L. hengyangensis, 239t
   L. hopelensis. See L. mantschurica
   L. intermedia, 239t
   L. kudoii, 239t
   L. mantschurica, **143**, 239t
   L. orientalis, 239t
   L. pellegrini, 239t
   L. posterodorsalis, 240t
   L. rubrilabris, 240t
   L. taeniops, 240t
   L. tchangi, 240t
   L. tientainensis, 240t
   L. zebra, 240t
lifespan of *Chromobotia macracanthus* (Clown loach), 107
lift, in movement of fishes, 176–178

Photo Credits